The
Handbook of
PROJECT
MANAGEMENT

A Practical Guide to Effective
Policies and Procedures

TREVOR L. YOUNG

The
Handbook of
PROJECT
MANAGEMENT

A Practical Guide to Effective
Policies and Procedures

TREVOR L. YOUNG

KOGAN
PAGE

YOURS TO HAVE AND TO HOLD
BUT NOT TO COPY

First published in 1996

Kogan Page Limited
120 Pentonville Road
London N1 9JN

© Trevor L Young, 1996

British Library Cataloguing in Publication Data
A CIP record for this book is available from the British Library.
ISBN   0 7494 1945 8

Typeset by Photoprint, Torquay, Devon
Printed and bound in Great Britain by Biddles Ltd, Guildford and Kings Lynn

CONTENTS

1. Introduction   9
   What is special about projects?   10
   Who is this book for?   10

2. Change and Projects   13
   Change and the project manager   14
   What is a project?   15
   How are projects derived?   16
   The dynamic lifecycle of a project   19
   The project dynamic action cycle   20
   What is project management?   21
   What is different about project management?   22
   Summary   23

3. The Project Manager's Role   25
   The project organisation   26
   The project manager as a leader   31
   Projects and teamwork   39
   Summary   43

4. Starting Up Your Project   45
   Information review   45
   Customer satisfaction   47
   Customer needs and expectations   48
   The customer contract   50
   Identifying the project constraints   50
   The kick-off meeting   51
   Project documentation   55
   The project brief and specification   59
   Summary   60

5. Defining Your Project   63
   What is necessary to define a project?   64
   The stakeholder list   64

The project brief   67
The scope of work statement   70
Risk management   71
Risk assessment   73
Ranking of risks identified   75
Risk monitoring   77
Getting your project definition approved   80
Summary   83

6. Planning Your Project   **85**
Where does planning start?   87
Identifying the key stages   89
The project work breakdown structure   93
Allocating responsibility   95
What is an estimate?   98
Estimating the durations   99
Contingencies   101
Time limited scheduling and estimates   102
Identifying the critical path of your project   103
The programme evaluation and review technique   105
Analysing the logic diagram   107
Using the PERT analysis data   107
Analyse your resource requirements   113
Optimising your schedule   114
Review your project risk log   116
Review your project budget   117
Seeking appoval to launch your project   117
Summary   120

7. Launching Your Project   **121**
Establishing key stage work plans   121
Establishing a milestone schedule   124
Critical success factors   127
Ensuring effective communication   128
Project status reports   129
Derive a meetings schedule for your project   132
Handling project changes   133
Hold a launch meeting   134
Summary   136

8. Executing the Project Work   **139**
The project control system   140
Monitoring progress   143
Managing issues   148
Tracking your project   150

Taking corrective action 156
Problem-solving 157
Progress meetings 161
Progress reporting 164
Projects and conflict 165
Managing time 169
Controlling the project costs 178
Summary 182

9. **Closing Your Project** 185
The acceptance process 186
The close-out meeting 187
Evaluating your project 190
Post-project appraisals 196
What next? 196
Summary 197

10. **Using a Computer** 201
What can software do? 202
What software does not do 206
Selecting project software 207

Postscript 209

Appendix 1: Glossary of Terms 211
Appendix 2: Further Reading 217

Index 219

1

INTRODUCTION

During the past decade the skills of project management have become increasingly recognised as highly desirable for managers at all levels in an organisation. Most people today can benefit from the application of these skills to some parts of their daily operations. The rapid growth of global markets and the introduction of total quality management, continuous improvement programmes and more recently the drive to redesign business processes all require these skills to some degree. All are aimed at improving organisational effectiveness and performance in a highly competitive world marketplace. The world marketplace is continually changing and every organisation, irrespective of their service or product, must accept that internal change is a normal process to meet the demands of external change.

The successful and effective implementation of change employs specific skills that have been traditionally owned by a select group of technical professionals. This is no longer true and the skills of managing change are essential for everyone in an organisation at all levels. Change always requires a cultural shift for everyone:

- introducing new processes;
- finding new and better procedures and working practices;
- throwing off the old habits to create a more dynamic and flexible organisation;
- ability to react effectively to market forces;
- ways to maintain competitiveness;
- ways to seek new horizons.

To carry out such change requires some special skills. Project management provides a structured and organised way to achieve success every time.

WHAT IS SPECIAL ABOUT PROJECTS?

If you ask anyone what is special about projects, expect to get a confused variation of responses. The Channel Tunnel, Concorde, North Sea oil rigs, motorways, inner city development, landing on the Moon, the Taj Mahal, the Pyramids and countless others are readily recognised as 'projects'. Certainly all can be termed 'special' – all have a clearly recognisable specific result at the point of completion and we can see the result thanks to the use of modern technology and communications. Each is unique and unlikely to be repeated again in quite the same way with identical results. These large undertakings involve a wide range of technical skills and often large numbers of people. At the other end of the spectrum many unique but much smaller undertakings occur in every type of organisation, that use fewer people but still require many skills to produce a desired result. All these activities involve change since they are concerned to create something that does not yet exist. The sum of the activities directed towards a specific result is regarded as a 'project'.

Such activities are frequently carried out outside the normal operations that keeps the mainstream activity of the organisation moving to satisfy its customers. It is seen as a burden on people demanding valuable time and resources. It incurs a commitment of expenditure of today's profits to generate future enhanced performance and benefits.

WHO IS THIS BOOK FOR?

Anyone involved in projects, regardless of their status or role in an organisation, will benefit from reading this book. But that is not the real purpose. The book is written to give you, the project manager, a guide to help you improve performance using well tried and tested tools and techniques. The skills of project management are not the only tools you will need to become a better project manager, yet many of these tools are valuable in your everyday work. It is clearly recognised that you do not spend all your time managing projects and it is more likely to be an occasional responsibility at some time in your career.

The book has been carefully designed to meet your needs if:

■ you are looking to develop the skills of effective project management to help you in your work as a member of a project team;

- you are about to start work on a project, having just been appointed to the role of project manager;
- you have managed projects already, but seek to improve your skills and welcome an opportunity to review your present knowledge, add some new tools and techniques to your portfolio and improve your performance;
- you have an involvement in projects and need to coach others in the application of project tools and techniques and the project process.

This is not an academic textbook offering you complex theories to learn. The tools and techniques of effective and successful project management are practical and relatively simple to understand. This does not mean they are always easy to apply due to the complexity of project work and the effects of scale. The emphasis is on business projects, which are often small and of short duration when compared to highly technical or construction projects.

The book is written as a pocket guide so it is not a book to read once and place in the bottom drawer of your desk, never to see the light of day again! The guide is a tool to be used frequently to help, remind and support what you do at each step along the road from start-up of a project through to successful completion. Throughout you will find practical tips and checklists for each step to help achieve the results expected.

2

CHANGE AND PROJECTS

Change in today's world affects everyone. You face a changing environment both in your private life as well as the business world in which you work. Some of these changes are beyond your control, such as the weather which not only changes with the passing seasons, but as many will tell you is changing in its behaviour with the passing years. Not all change is so automatic and uncontrolled. You can choose to create change in your life by taking carefully designed decisions. You choose to change jobs, move house, or adopt a different lifestyle as an expression of your personal desires and as a means of satisfying your current needs. Frequently you face changes that you do not choose because the decision is taken by another. You do not like an increase in taxation but someone decides it is essential for the greater good of the economy. Such change is obligatory for all and you have to face consequential changes and take decisions to further adapt your lifestyle to accommodate the reduction in income. Similarly others at work take decisions about how you must work or what you do. You have no input to the change and you are expected to accept the new environment that results. Technological advances continue to affect you at an increasing pace, creating additional stress through the need to keep up to date. Much of this change is a subtle, cumulative process that erodes the comfortable habits you have created over time, disturbing the normality and stability of familiarity. One thing is a certainty, the pace of change will continue to increase in the future. Your response determines your effectiveness in managing the process rather than letting the change manage you!

The consequences of change are either perceived as trivial or range through to very significant, affecting your response. Success in managing change is directly related to your ability to:

- understand the current reality;
- carefully design the change process;
- manage the consequences.

These processes help you to accept any change as an opportunity and a challenge. When you choose a change, you are positive and constructive about the consequences even if things do not work out as you expected. But an imposed change often creates negative and critical responses with open opposition and even attempts to sabotage the desired results. Such reactions can occur regardless of the value of the change. The result is an impact on how the change process is managed to achieve a successful outcome.

CHANGE AND THE PROJECT MANAGER

If you are to be successful in your management of change then you need to have a set of proven tools and techniques at your disposal to support your efforts. You cannot afford to ignore the nature of change and the impact on people, their reactions, fears and concerns about the future. The project is concerned with creating change in an organised and structured manner. As the project manager, achieving success is a measure of your ability to become an effective change agent.

You are faced with dealing with the fears that act to restrain the change process. At the same time you demonstrate your enthusiasm and excitement at the prospect of achieving advances in the way your organisation operates in the current and future business environment. This demands a wide range of people skills besides those traditionally associated with managing projects. These include:

- setting clear objectives and aligning people's personal goals;
- creating a real sense of responsibility and obligation in the project team;
- managing a team as an interactive unit;
- creating a sense of commitment in the team members, some of whom may have little interest in the results expected;
- coaching, guiding and actively supporting the individual team members;
- explaining decisions and keeping everyone informed of progress;
- establishing a sustaining environment for effective dialogue and feedback in the team and with other teams and their management;
- managing upwards to influence senior management and other line managers;
- managing third parties – contractors, suppliers, consultants;

- understanding the real needs of the end users of the results;
- satisfying the internal customer;
- handling conflicts effectively;
- demonstrating a concern for continuous improvement, questioning traditions and always seeking a better way of doing things;
- taking a holistic view – seeing the bigger picture, understanding where the change fits into corporate strategy, other project activity, expected future changes.

This list may seem formidable, putting unexpected demands on your current skills. As a project manager these are skills you will learn and improve as you become a more effective agent of change.

WHAT IS A PROJECT?

In most organisations the process of maintaining normal operations to meet the corporate objectives is the primary responsibility of the functional management. This includes the activities associated with improving effectiveness on a day-to-day basis through continuous improvement, seeking always to be better at the way the essential work is carried out. You recognise this is the traditional way to get things done because it is dependent on the habits and working practices generated by experience.

The project provides the organisation with an alternative way of achieving results where the work to be done is likely to cross functional boundaries. It involves people in different parts or divisions of an organisation, even different sites in the same or different countries. This allows you to use the most appropriate skills, gathered into a coordinated work unit, to achieve results that would be difficult to accomplish in one department. The idea is not new, since most large pieces of work such as construction activities have always required a diverse range of particular skills. These skills are not within the capability of one individual.

The rapid advance of modern technology has created an enormous group of specialists, each with experience and extensive knowledge needed for the work. Even the smallest project today may call for this experience and knowledge from technologists, engineers, scientists, finance specialists, marketers, sales people and others.

Your job as the project manager is to obtain the services of these specialists, from wherever they work in the organisation, to achieve a successful outcome. The project is a powerful mechanism for achieving that success.

The project is therefore something special by its nature and is perceived as being an activity outside normal operations. It is defined as:

> ... *a collection of linked activities, carried out in an organised manner with a clearly defined start point and finish point, to achieve some specific results that satisfy the needs of an organisation as derived from the current business plans.*

Because it is a practical activity carried out beyond normal operations you will need to use a different approach to the work involved to achieve the desired results. The most unusual element of the project work is the particular effort you must use to manage a team, whose membership is subject to continual change due to:

- the range of skills required at any particular time;
- the availability of individuals in different departments, each of which has continually changing priorities.

It is difficult enough for you to build an effective team in a hierarchical structure with dedicated full-time members. Add the transitory nature of the project team and the job has increased complexity. You have to give additional attention to the essential skills of communication, negotiation and influencing others to keep everyone's focus on the project objectives.

The main characteristics of project are listed in Figure 2.1.

HOW ARE PROJECTS DERIVED?

As you have seen the project is a vehicle for carrying change to its intended conclusion to give your organisation something it does not currently have, but is strongly desired. But from where do the ideas come for all this project activity? You may feel the answer is obvious – the senior management maybe. Anyone in the organisation may come up with the ideas for a project. Creativity and idea generation are not the exclusive territory of the management. It is the people who do the day-to-day operational work who often have the best ideas to improve organisational performance. To identify how projects are derived it is appropriate to examine their sources in the organisation (see Figure 2.2).

Every organisation today engages in business planning in some manner – this is commonly a three- or five-year corporate plan and a shorter one-year strategic plan. The corporate plan will set the

---

THE CHARACTERISTICS OF PROJECTS

A project:

- has a specific purpose which can be readily defined;
- is unique because it is most unlikely to be repeated in exactly the same way by the same group of people to give the same results;
- is focused on the customer and customer expectations;
- is not usually routine work but may include routine type tasks;
- is made up of a collection of activities that are linked together because they all contribute to the desired result;
- has clearly defined and agreed time constraints – a date when the results are required;
- is frequently complex because the work involves people in different departments and even on different sites;
- has to be flexible to accommodate change as the work proceeds;
- involves many unknowns both within the work itself, the skills of the people doing the work and the external influences on the project;
- has cost constraints which must be clearly defined and understood to ensure the project remains viable at all times;
- provides a unique opportunity to learn new skills;
- forces you to work in a different way because the 'temporary' management role is directly associated with the life of the project;
- challenges traditional lines of authority with perceived threats to the status quo;
- involves risk at every step of the process and you must manage these risks to sustain the focus on the desired results.

Figure 2.1 *Project characteristics.*

future direction of the organisation and establish broad targets to meet. The strategic plan is a more detailed documentation of how the organisation will meet the corporate plan through the next year.

The majority of the effort will be directed towards achieving the operational targets for the year. Everyone whose job contributes to achieving the growth set out in the strategy seeks to improve performance. Continuous improvement is not an initiative or campaign but should be part of everyday work and a way of life for everyone, seeking always to find better ways to do the job to make the organisation more effective and more efficient. Sometimes good ideas that come from continuous improvement activity

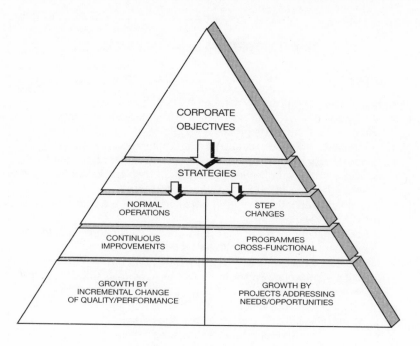

Figure 2.2 *Sources of projects.*

in one part of the organisation may have benefits to other functions. This may then require a considerable effort with a cross-functional team to make a significant change effectively. The organisation can gain considerably from treating this type of continuous improvement as a project, because of the size and complexity of the work involved.

Most project activity in an organisation starts by someone recognising the importance of addressing specific needs or opportunities now to yield defined benefits. The purpose is to give the organisation something that does not yet exist but is clearly defined as essential or highly desirable to support the process of achieving the strategic plan for the year. Some projects may be of longer life and directed towards the corporate objectives within the three- or five-year plan. It may be considered necessary to start a programme comprising several projects that are connected by a common overall objective, eg a cost reduction programme. All have one important characteristic – they involve a step change or quantum leap from current business process or operations. They are directly derived from the organisation's vision for the future and form a significant contribution towards achieving that vision.

How does this affect you as the project manager? You have an interest in success and a key element of success is the project team, ie the people doing the work. It is not enough to just hand out the work you decide is necessary for the project. The people in the team must participate in all aspects of the work from the start-up and definition through to completion. You can get the team motivated, enthusiastic about the work and focused on the objectives if you can explain the context of the project in the organisation's strategy. Then everyone understands why the project exists, its importance and relative priority compared with other work.

Occasionally you may be faced with a mandatory project. This is a change controlled by an external requirement such as new UK legislation, EU Directives or health and safety requirements. Such projects often do not arouse enthusiasm but are still important for the organisation and are always part of strategy. After all, failure to comply may lead to legal and commercial difficulties or financial penalties.

THE DYNAMIC LIFECYCLE OF A PROJECT

Because the project has such specific characteristics, all limited by time, it naturally goes through a lifecycle just like a product. The difference with a project is that the lifecycle is dynamic and subject to reiteration at any time during the project.

The front end of any project is marked by the initial decision to proceed. This start-up is often very 'woolly' and ill-defined and is discussed in more detail in Chapter 4.

All projects go through a similar lifecycle, comprising four fundamental phases:

- *Phase 1 – Definition*. The start of the project once needs have been clearly identified and the project can be defined with the agreement of those people with an interest in the outcomes.
- *Phase 2 – Planning*. The process of planning the project to derive a realistic schedule taking into account the constraints imposed on the project.
- *Phase 3 – Execution*. Launching the project work ensuring everyone understands the plan, the controls you impose on the process and making sure the plan is always up to date with any changes that occur.

■ *Phase 4 – Closure*. Preparing your customer for acceptance and handover to ensure the project has delivered the agreed outcomes, any follow-on activities are identified and assigned and the project evaluation process is completed.

THE PROJECT DYNAMIC ACTION CYCLE

In practice these four phases are only a convenience for you to separate the project work into blocks with a defined sequence. The reality is that no project follows such a neat and simple process flow without a significant amount of reiteration. At any stage of the project work you may have to:

■ revise the project definition;
■ replan part of the work;
■ revise the project schedule;
■ solve problems;
■ carry out recovery planning – to recover lost time;
■ carry out contingency planning – in case a high-risk part of the work goes wrong.

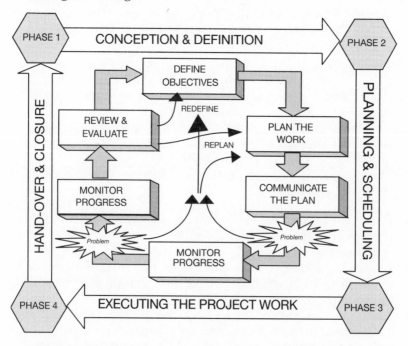

Figure 2.3 *The four phases and the dynamic action cycle.*

The *action cycle* gives the basic steps a project (or any part of a project) must go through with the four phases identified earlier. Figure 2.3 shows the cycle in a graphic form.

At each of the steps it may become necessary to recycle the process and redo some of the work. This reiteration throughout the project process maintains the project dynamics. It provides a check that you are doing the right things to keep the project on track to the schedule and achieve the desired outcomes agreed with your customer.

WHAT IS PROJECT MANAGEMENT?

The management of your project is essentially the control system you use to achieve the right results or outcomes. The four phases and the action cycle comprise the dynamic process you are going to employ, so project management is defined as:

> ... *the dynamic process utilising the appropriate resources of the organisation in a controlled and structured manner, employed to achieve a change clearly defined with* **specific objectives** *identified as strategic needs.*

The process is always associated with some specific characteristics:

- *objectives oriented* – without these you have no outcomes;
- *change oriented* – creating something you need but do not have;
- *multi-disciplined* – needs a wide range of skills to achieve success;
- *opportunistic* – you must seek to take shortcuts and bypass old norms;
- *performance oriented* – setting appropriate standards and quality of outputs;
- *control oriented* – carefully designed controls to maintain the schedule;
- *questions tradition* – avoid getting trapped by the old ways of doing things.

Too often the selection of team members for a project team is controlled less by the skill set needed and more by 'who is available'. Always ensure you have some part in the selection process. You probably will not have a free hand to select who you want but at least you can exert a strong influence. Many projects have run into difficulties because the wrong team was selected at the outset. If project management is accepted as an essential skill in your organisation you will find it possible to influence senior managers to support your efforts from the beginning.

WHAT IS DIFFERENT ABOUT PROJECT MANAGEMENT?

The principal difference is that you are operating in a temporary role. You are only the manager of the project team for the life of the project and then you return to your other operational duties – or another project with possibly a different team. This situation leads to some specific differences when compared to the 'fixed' hierarchical team that is part of the organisational structure.

In a fixed team as the manager you:

- lead the team;
- have team members reporting direct to you alone;
- have a stable team membership, medium to long term;
- create the conditions for good teamworking;
- set the team norms and behaviours with the team;
- decide responsibilities and coach team members in new skills;
- control the work of the team – input and output;
- build trust and respect in the team;
- encourage personal growth and development of the team members;
- encourage sharing of information, opinions and feelings for the team's benefit;
- utilise the team's creative skills to improve team performance;
- appraise the team members' performance;
- set individual targets to improve performance;
- create a team identity.

The project team you bring together will almost certainly have come from different departments in the organisation, maybe even different sites. Although you must attempt to do all the things just listed you will have difficulty with some.

- Team members only report to you for their work on the project but report to their line manager for other work – unless they are fully dedicated to the project.
- Your team membership is less likely to have stability due to changing priorities of the team members' line managers.
- With a changing team membership, conditions for good teamwork are more difficult to create.

- Often team members do not know each other and team norms take a considerable time to develop.
- You are in a time limited situation and can find little time for coaching – you need the skills immediately.
- Team members who do not know each other well are always hesitant to share information, opinions and feelings openly.
- You can only appraise an individual on their project work – remember they may be working on more than one project at a time for different project managers and still have line responsibilities. So who does their appraisal and how?
- Creating a team identity requires time and additional effort on your part to ensure the team comes together regularly as a team to learn more about each other.

The organisational hierarchical structure is a matrix from which your team is drawn and during the early stages of a project everyone is getting used to the situation of working with a different group of people. This can lead to more conflict than you would like so pay particular attention to getting to know and understand the team members yourself through setting up regular one-to-one meetings with each.

Success in project management is not going to be yours by just using the right tools and techniques. It is only achieved through giving time to leading the team and overcoming these areas of potential difficulty. This will then reduce the risk of failure.

SUMMARY

- *Projects are an essential part of a change process.*

- *Projects are a means to*:
    - achieve step changes;
    - continuously improve business performance;
    - involve people across the organisation;
    - break down functional barriers.

- *Projects*:
    - depend on people and teamwork;
    - are unique activities;
    - are concerned to create something that does not yet exist;
    - have specific and desired outcomes with clear benefits;
    - are subject to risk.

- *All projects follow a dynamic lifecycle:*
  - definition;
  - planning;
  - execution;
  - closure.

- *Project management is different from other management roles:*
  - it is a temporary role;
  - the team membership is flexible and changes as project needs vary;
  - it is a time and resource limited activity.

3

THE PROJECT MANAGER'S ROLE

As a project manager you are now aware that it is a complex role. It does not have the perceived security of a steady-state situation. You are submerged in a change environment and your primary purpose is to achieve a successful outcome from the project. You are in a difficult temporary management role with specific responsibilities that are linked only to the project. These are not normal in a team role or as leader of a permanent team in the organisation's hierarchy.

You have to create a balance between the demands and needs of:

- the customer;
- the project;
- the organisation;
- the project team.

You must do everything you believe necessary out of concern for the project and eventual success. This means it is not a recipe for a quiet life! You know your organisation and the people with whom you are expecting to work and might expect opposition, conflict, subtle interference and even outright sabotage! Of course, these things never happen in your organisation so you always expect full cooperation, enthusiastic support, strong commitment and plenty of helpful advice. The reality is somewhere in between these two extremes, sometimes tending to one extreme or the other.

Your skills are tested to the full with the wide range of activities you have to accomplish to preserve the integrity of your project at all times. If you are not assigned full time to the role you also have to balance the time between project activities and your other duties. This really tests your ability as a time manager that may influence your team members who are in a similar situation.

As the project manager you are:

- responsible for achieving a successful outcome;
- delighting your customer;
- expected to have proven skills in the use of project tools and techniques;
- expected to have proven team leadership skills;
- limited in authority to secure resources, internally and externally;
- forced to cut through hierarchical boundaries to get things done;
- expected to work with established working practices and customs;
- working with the unknown and unpredictable;
- in a position subject to risk;
- regarded with distrust by many of those not involved.

All of these elements demand and extend leadership skills beyond those normally associated with a fixed team leadership role. The project manager's lot is a lonely one! You are slipped sideways from your line management position in the hierarchy to allow you to use all the appropriate skills from across the organisation to achieve success.

THE PROJECT ORGANISATION

A project organisation is commonly established by default through a decision taken at an executive level to initiate a project. This leads to a project manager being appointed and a 'core team' being assigned to the project. The team members are often selected because of their availability or previous project experience and are likely to be associated with the project for all or most of its life. The project manager and the core team are unlikely to be dedicated full time to the project unless it is very significant. They will have other work or project activity as part of their everyday obligations (see Figure 3.1).

Most organisations are organised by function – sales, marketing, production, finance, personnel, etc. For many projects the core team are not necessarily drawn from one functional area and similarly the 'extended team' are drawn from across the functional structure. This extended team are those individuals who only have membership of the project team for a relatively short time to do a specific part of the project work. This approach to establishing the

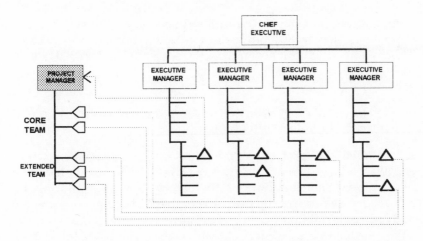

Figure 3.1 *Organisation structure for projects.*

project team is the same for a full-time dedicated team as well as a part-time team who have other responsibilities.

Usually many projects are 'active' or considered to be active so there is a complex matrix of project teams distributed within the functional hierarchy. This situation encourages:

- uncertain lines of accountability;
- unclear responsibilities – who is responsible for what?;
- poor project control – most will be late or delayed;
- unclear view of resource utilisation leading to individual overload;
- no prioritisation of project activity from an organisational overview position;
- 'projects' being initiated at random at all levels and often hidden from view;
- a belief that projects need 100 per cent dedicated teams for success.

Creating a structure for ownership

To overcome these problems created by the confusion of many projects supposedly 'active' requires a clearly defined project organisation structure that is overlaid on the functional hierarchy. To ensure that all the potentially 'active' projects in the organisation are adequately resourced would usually require a significant increase in staff numbers!

As you saw in Chapter 2 all project activity is directed towards supporting the overall purpose of meeting corporate objectives. This is either within normal operations or to achieve the step changes desired by the organisation. This can only be successfully achieved through:

... a clear definition of ownership at each level in the organisation with clearly defined roles and responsibilities.

It is essential that projects are not initiated as a management whim at any level but are only allowed when it is demonstrated they make a clear contribution to corporate strategy. This can only be achieved if senior management is involved in the project process and has responsibilities which are clearly defined for the 'sponsorship' of all project activity. The sponsors come from this senior management group where authority should be clearly defined. The project sponsors can operate individually or as a group to form a project steering team, ensuring everyone in the organisation focuses on the important active projects (see Figure 3.2).

This ensures a clear decision process exists on all aspects of project work and you have a clear understanding to whom you are reporting. It also creates a clear sense of direction for all project activity in the organisation and prioritises projects for the limited available resources.

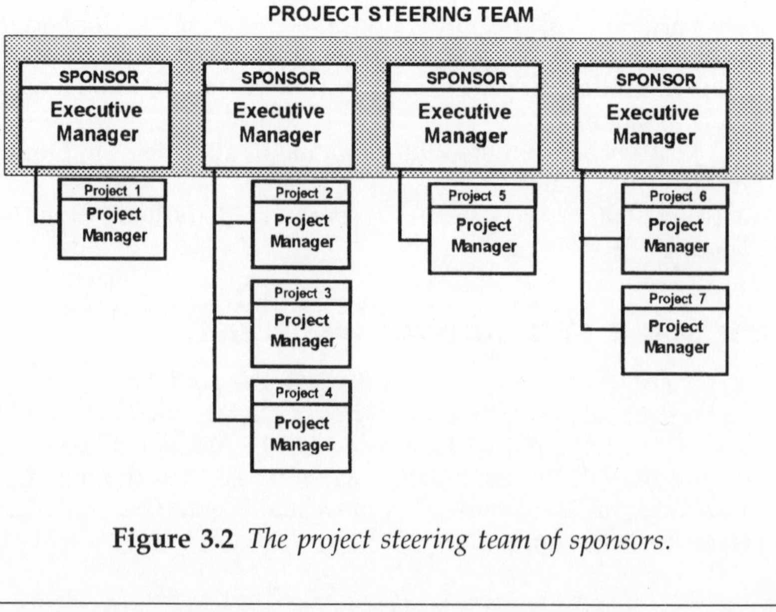

PROJECT STEERING TEAM

Figure 3.2 *The project steering team of sponsors.*

Project steering team

This group of project sponsors – the project steering team (PST) – meets at regular intervals to review the status of all active projects, initiate new projects and decide the prioritisation of project activity in the organisation. Responsibilities include:

- ensuring projects are aligned to corporate objectives;
- giving strategic direction;
- maintaining focus on customer and business needs;
- ensuring environmental influences are taken into account (internal and external);
- prioritising all active projects and their resourcing;
- resolving escalated issues;
- providing the ultimate decision forum for all major problems and issues;
- approving start-up and abortion of projects.

Project sponsor

The project sponsor for any project is accountable (to the PST) for the performance of their projects and must demonstrate their concern for success to everyone involved. Responsibilities include:

- ensuring project objectives are always aligned to corporate needs;
- selecting the project manager;
- approving the project definition;
- sustaining the project direction;
- ensuring priorities are maintained for all their projects;
- overseeing the project process and procedures, budget and control;
- reacting promptly to issues escalated to them for decisions;
- maintaining support and commitment;
- approving project plans, changes and status reports.

The project manager

The project manager is responsible for the project work from the initial kick-off through to closure. Responsibilities include:

- selecting the core team with the project sponsor;
- identifying and managing the project stakeholders;
- defining the project and securing stakeholder approval;

- planning the project and securing stakeholder approval;
- identifying and managing the risks;
- allocating and securing resource commitments;
- monitoring and tracking project progress;
- solving the problems that interfere with progress;
- controlling costs;
- leading the project team;
- informing stakeholders of progress status;
- delivering the project deliverables and benefits;
- managing the performance of everyone involved with the project.

A new term has appeared here – the *stakeholders*. These are the people who have a specific and clearly definable interest in your project – a stake in gambling terms! They are an important group of people as we see a little later in this chapter.

Of course only the primary responsibilities are given in the lists above, and they can be expanded considerably for a particular organisation. All of these roles are important to success in project work. You can see how a coordinated project community can develop in the organisation and you are part of that structure now as a project manager. It is appropriate to define some other terms you use frequently in managing a project:

Responsibility
The obligation to ensure the project tasks or a piece of work are carried out efficiently, to the relevant quality standards and on time.

Your role demands that you create a climate in your team where responsibility is clearly defined and accepted. Without acceptance there is no commitment and the work is not done well or willingly.

Responsibility is discrete to an individual and cannot be shared – a shared or split responsibility is no responsibility and generates a blame culture!

Authority
The right to take and implement management decisions.

You can make decisions – it is just a process of generating options for a solution to a problem. You need authority to decide which to use and then implement the selected option. This authority is normally confined to taking decisions about people, equipment, materials and money. All these areas, directly or indirectly, involve spending or saving money and you must have a clear understanding about your limits. It is not common practice to define these limits in writing.

It is a good idea to get a clear statement of authority from your project sponsor, specific to the project work only. Make sure other managers are informed of the authority given to you for the project. This can support your efforts and improve cooperation once the real project work starts. You are expected to take technical decisions based on your knowledge and experience – or based on that in the team.

Authority clearly defined and delegated at the outset speeds decisions and improves the probability of success. It is an essential part of empowerment.

Accountability
The management control over authority.

When you are given authority you are held to account for its effective use – and abuse! No authority means no accountability. If you fail to achieve a task on time, you have not fulfilled your obligations and therefore not carried out your responsibility effectively. Responsibility is often confused with accountability, which is used as a threatening word to emphasise priority or the importance of some work.

Accountability is the partner of authority – you are only accountable for the use of management authority that is given by delegation.

Confusion tends to occur about accountability for technical decisions. If you use your technical knowledge and skills when taking a decision, then you are accountable for that part that is purely technical. If money is involved and outside your authority then you must refer to your project sponsor to take the decision.

THE PROJECT MANAGER AS A LEADER

To achieve success in your project you need to use a collection of skills that demonstrates your ability to lead a team. You are

---

QUALITIES OF AN EFFECTIVE PROJECT LEADER

A list of desirable qualities includes:

- flexibility and adaptability;
- demonstration of significant initiative;
- assertiveness, confidence and verbal fluency;
- ambition, drive and commitment;
- effective communicator and good listener;
- enthusiasm, imagination and creativity;
- well organised and self-disciplined;
- a generalist rather than a specialist – has technical awareness;
- able to identify and facilitate problem-solving;
- able to make and take decisions promptly;
- promotes a motivating climate;
- keeps everyone focused on the project objectives;
- trained in project management tools and techniques;
- experienced in project management processes and procedures;
- respected by peers and management;
- concerned to achieve success.

Figure 3.3 *Qualities of the project leader.*

working with and through others, using these skills to energise and direct a diverse group of people to give a high performance, willingly and enthusiastically throughout the project. These people come from different parts of the organisation, each of which has its own culture through the leadership style of the departmental manager. You have to overcome these cultural variations to create a climate of cooperation and coordinate the efforts of the team members without direct line authority.

Much has been written about leadership, the skills required and an appropriate style for different types of work. There is a diverse range of opinions about what makes an 'effective leader'. There are no common characteristics that you must have to be effective, and without which you are doomed to fail. At the core of leadership is your skill at influencing the behaviour of people to achieve your objectives. Figure 3.3 lists some of the qualities one might expect to find in a project leader.

One extreme of leadership style is the autocrat, where you tell people what to do using a 'you will' approach. The other extreme is the democrat, where information is shared, you consult widely and ask people to do the work using a 'will you' approach. The reality is you adopt a style that is often subconsciously directed by:

- the situation and the prevailing environment;
- the type of work, its priority and urgency;
- the way the team reacts and behaves in the environment.

When a crisis hits, many people will tend to adopt a more autocratic style in the interests of getting a quick result. It is perceived that no time exists for consultation, ideas and suggestions are not encouraged and consensus is avoided. The actions required are dictated by command and control. The democratic style is regarded as slower, encouraging people to give their ideas and opinions, always seeking a consensus so the team is fully involved and well motivated to achieve results.

What is appropriate for the role of project manager? There is no 'right' style – only a style that seems to work and that is appropriate with the people at the time. Your real skill as a leader is your ability to recognise what approach is appropriate at any particular time to get results. A project is a very specialised situation because of:

- the nature of the work, which is time and cost constrained;
- the diverse range of skills and experience of people you do not know well.

To achieve the project objectives you must use some particular skills to:

- ensure the project tasks are completed on time to the quality desired;
- create coordination between the team members and develop teamwork;
- support the individual team members and develop their skills for the project.

These three elements of the leadership role are related and interdependent and you cannot ignore any one at the expense of the others. They are all directed in one fundamental direction – the project objectives.

Keeping a balance between these three elements occupies much of your time as the leader. The actions you take at each stage of the project are focused on maintaining this balance, adopting a range of styles according to the prevailing situation. However, in any project the people involved are not just yourself and the team. You have a *customer* – the person or group of people who expect to receive the outcomes – and a *project sponsor* who is accountable for the project results. There are also many others who have an interest in the journey you are going to take. This is the *stakeholder* group.

The project stakeholders

Anyone in the organisation who potentially at some time has an interest in your project is a stakeholder. You need to identify these people because they are certain to attempt to exert influence about how you manage the project. The team members come from different departments and their line managers have agreed to losing their resource for some of the working weeks ahead. The line managers are often *key stakeholders* – they can have a significant impact on your project if their priorities change and you lose a promised resource. Other *key stakeholders* include:

■ your customer;
■ your project sponsor;
■ the customer's user group;
■ the finance department.

Many other people or departments across the organisation will consider they have a stake – production, quality, accounts, test, sales, marketing, personnel. If they do have a stake you must consult them to determine their interest and how it may influence your project. All stakeholders have a hidden agenda about what they expect from your project and you need to expose these expectations before you define the project. This is not always easy where there is a political dimension to stakeholder needs and expectations – one need could be to hinder or stop the project!

Stakeholders are not only inside the organisation. Many external people are expecting to have work from your project – suppliers, contractors, consultants and possibly government departments or agencies.

All have their reasons for becoming involved in the project. You have no authority over any of your stakeholders and it is a formidable challenge to manage them effectively and gain their help and support.

The dimensions of project leadership

You can now see that the role of project manager is complex, managing a team and a diverse group of other people to achieve the project objectives. Figure 3.4 shows the relationship between the key elements of leadership, the project objectives and the stakeholders.

You spend much of your time *inner directed*, focusing on the project tasks, developing and maintaining good teamwork and making sure you have the right skills in the team. You also spend time *outer directed*, spending time with your stakeholders to understand their needs and expectations, using their skills when appropriate and keeping them informed of progress.

You cannot ignore your stakeholders, you must manage them. They can influence your project at any time with serious conse-

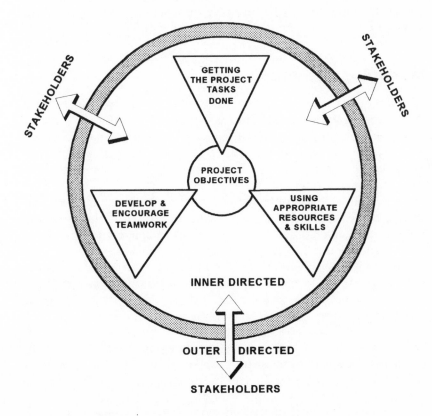

Figure 3.4 *The project leader's relationships.*

quences to progress. They can change their minds at any time, cause delays and demand changes to your plans.

In Chapter 2 you looked at the characteristics of a project and the project dynamic lifecycle. This dynamic cycle of actions throughout the project is one of the three essential dimensions of project leadership:

■ identifying and managing the project stakeholders throughout the project life;
■ managing the project dynamic lifecycle from definition through planning and execution to closure – all the tasks of the project;
■ managing the performance of yourself, the team and the stakeholders.

Success with your project is directly related to balancing the time and effort you give to each of these dimensions from the start-up until you hand over the results to your customer.

Managing stakeholders

Identifying stakeholders is not just part of the project start-up. Many do not appear until later so you must review your list of stakeholders at regular intervals. The relative importance of each changes with time and the stages of the project. If you fail to recognise or cooperate with any stakeholder you take a serious risk. That stakeholder could force views or changes to your plans at a time that is least convenient to you and hinders progress. You are the project manager and must set the ground rules from the outset. Poor stakeholder control can lead to chaos and demotivation of your team!

Ask your project sponsor to inform all your internal stakeholders about the strategic importance and priority of your project. This makes your job easier when you approach them later for active support of your efforts. Many of the stakeholders have valuable knowledge and experience. If appropriate use this experience for your project and seek their input when you feel it can help the team. You can even bring a stakeholder into the 'extended team' for a time if he or she can make a specific contribution.

You need stakeholder support and commitment always, so part of your tactics is to feed that support using diplomacy and tact. You are the project manager so they must understand your responsibilities and accept you are in charge of the daily work of the team. You welcome positive suggestions and ideas and do not want covert criticism or interference that demotivates the team, destroys team spirit and promotes conflict.

CHECKLIST 1: IDENTIFYING AND MANAGING STAKEHOLDERS

Identify all potential stakeholders:

- Recognise which are the key stakeholders.
- Divide the list into internal and external.
- What needs to be known about each stakeholder?
- Where and how can information be gathered?
- Gather information about each:
  - What exactly is the interest?
  - Why are they interested?
  - What are they expecting to gain?
  - How will the project affect them?
  - Can they contribute valuable experience or knowledge?
  - What are their strengths and weaknesses?
  - Are there hidden agendas?
  - What authority does the stakeholder have?
  - Does the stakeholder have legal rights?
  - Are they in favour of the project?
  - Will the project interfere with their operations?
  - Could they seriously hinder or block the project progress?
  - Is there any history of behaviour from previous projects?
- Who is entitled to see the information gathered?

Prepare a list of stakeholders, then:

- Assign responsibility for management of key stakeholders to yourself.
- Assign responsibility for management of other stakeholders to team members.
- Review and update the list at regular intervals.
- Distribute the list to all stakeholders to show you recognise their interest.
- Meet with them regularly to understand changes to their needs.
- Keep them informed of progress.
- Involve them in your decisions when appropriate.
- Make use of their skills and experience in the project.

Managing the project dynamic lifecycle

This involves you in controlling the project tasks, the resources needed to complete the tasks on time and all the materials and equipment required. You must control the project to stay on track to a schedule derived from the plan, dealing with changes, managing project risks and resolving issues that arise. Simultaneously you must demonstrate your concern for your team members and any other people engaged in carrying out the project work. They are looking to you as the leader of the team to provide them with a congenial working environment and to give support and guidance.

Chapters 4 to 9 take you through the lifecycle process and the actions you take as the project manager to achieve a successful oucome from your project.

Managing performance

As the project manager you must demonstrate throughout the project that you are concerned about the performance of everyone involved with the work of the project.

You are responsible for delivering the results expected by the key stakeholders and evaluating your performance regularly will help you improve the way you do the job. Project work requires effective teamwork. If the team is not well coordinated the project work suffers and you then jump from crisis to crisis. This is made more difficult because the team members often come from different departments or even other sites. You must make an effort early in the project to understand your team members and their working environment, what they hope to gain from the project and their personal objectives. The stakeholders provide the drive, direction and climate for success. Ignore them and you court potential disaster!

CHECKLIST 2: MANAGING PERFORMANCE

Evaluate your own performance continuously. Pay particular attention to:

- helping and supporting your team members;
- coaching individual team members when opportunities arise;
- responding promptly to personal issues raised with you;

- demonstrating your continued enthusiasm for the project;
- reviewing your decisions and being prepared to admit to mistakes if they happen;
- examining your management of time;
- evaluating your attention to detail in administering the project work;
- seeking external help when appropriate;
- avoiding the making of promises you cannot or do not intend to fulfil.

Work closely with your team to:

- understand their personal objectives;
- keep all the team involved and well informed;
- establish clear responsibilities for the work;
- act promptly when conflict appears;
- encourage good communication within the team and with their line managers;
- recognise team effort and high performance;
- look after the team's interests at all times in the interests of the project.

You must avoid continual firefighting so ensure you:

- keep key stakeholders regularly informed of progress;
- get them committed to their promises of support;
- involve them in important decisions when replanning or solving problems;
- monitor team members responsible for other stakeholders;
- encourage the team to maintain good communications with stakeholders.

PROJECTS AND TEAMWORK

Because most projects involve more than one person, teamwork is crucial to achieve success. To get effective teamwork you start by taking a group of people from different backgrounds, with different experience, skills and personal needs, and build them into a cohesive working unit. If the team members are only giving part of their working day or week to your project activities they have divided loyalties to different line managers and different working practices. The complexity increases if they are working in more than one project team at the same time.

The first time you bring your core team together they are really a group of individuals. They may not have worked with each other before even if they know one another. They come from different functions and their behaviour at work is conditioned by their normal operational environment. You are an unknown entity to them if they have not worked with you before. They expect you to break down the barriers and start to build the group into a team.

CHECKLIST 3: SELECTING TEAM MEMBERS

The criteria for selecting team members depends on the type of project. Ask:

- What is their relevant technical experience?
- Have they specialised knowledge essential to the project?
- Have they experience of similar projects?
- Have they worked in project teams before?
- Do they have relevant technical knowledge?
- What is their departmental authority?
- Have they other project commitments now?
- When do these commitments end?
- What is their capacity for project work (as a percentage of the working week)?
- What is their current non-project workload?
- Can this loading be reduced?
- What is their forecast future non-project workload?
- Can they be assigned for the whole project duration?
- Do they get on easily with other people?
- Do they like working alone?
- How do they feel about taking on a leadership role sometimes?
- Are they interested to join your team?
- What do they expect to gain from joining your team?
- Do they have a track record of commitment to high performance?
- Are they well organised and good time managers?
- Do they take their current responsibilities seriously?
- Are they perceived as good team players?
- Is their line manager in agreement with the possible assignment?

Availability is not an automatic guarantee to selection.

This is a complex process but it is made a little easier by having a clear sense of direction. Everyone should know why they are in the team – except that you selected them! They all have experience and skills you consider relevant to the project. Your objective is to harness their abilities, creativity and efforts to achieve a shared goal or outcome. If this potential is to benefit the organisation you must make sure you select the right team.

Selecting team members solely based on functional role is no guarantee the individual can effectively contribute to your project team. You must guard against the possibility that the setting up of a project team is not used as an opportunity by other managers to offer inexperienced team members. It is an exciting place to work and you want creative, enthusiastic people with a strong sense of responsibility and commitment. A successful team consists of a carefully designed mixture of the right skills and personalities who can work together without dissension and conflict. You select people for your team because you value and respect their ability to do a good job under pressure and not because you like them or they are popular!

A balanced team, encouraged to mature its working norms quickly, can overcome overwhelming difficulties and achieve what appears at times to be a 'Mission Impossible'.

Building your team

Clearly you face many potential difficulties in getting a project team working well. Do not despair. Many are normal in team development and often predictable. Team size can add to complexity if the team is large (more than five or six). Pay particular attention to avoiding:

- confusion over any aspect of the project;
- unclear responsibilities;
- unclear lines of authority;
- uneven workload distribution;
- unclear task assignments;
- unclear overall objectives;
- stakeholders not identified;
- communication breakdowns;
- mistrust between team members;
- personal objectives unrelated to project work;
- no commitment to project plan;
- no real team spirit;
- no concern about quality;
- a climate of suspicion;
- lack of direction;
- conflict and personality clashes;
- rigid attitudes.

There is no secret to success, no magic dust to sprinkle around to remove these difficulties if they occur. Take positive actions to minimise the problems and act promptly when necessary. You sometimes have to take unpopular decisions in the interests of the project. Test your team at intervals with the simple test in Figure 3.5. Check that teamworking improves as the project progresses – it's not about luck, it's just hard work!

Successful teams don't just happen, they have to be built through effective leadership and commitment.

HOW IS YOUR TEAM DOING?

Answer each statement with a ranking in the range 1–5.

The team knows exactly what it has to get done:
     Disagree strongly 1 2 3 4 5 Agree strongly

The team members are encouraged to offer ideas and suggestions:
     Disagree strongly 1 2 3 4 5 Agree strongly

The team members are encouraged to express their opinions freely and share information:
     Disagree strongly 1 2 3 4 5 Agree strongly

Each team member has a clear idea of their role and responsibilities in the project:
     Disagree strongly 1 2 3 4 5 Agree strongly

Everyone in the team is listened to with interest:
     Disagree strongly 1 2 3 4 5 Agree strongly

Everyone in the team is involved in making and taking decisions:
     Disagree strongly 1 2 3 4 5 Agree strongly

Team members do not feel threatened by exposing their true feelings:
     Disagree strongly 1 2 3 4 5 Agree strongly

The team members respect each other and encourage each other in their work:
     Disagree strongly 1 2 3 4 5 Agree strongly

Teamwork enables personal development and ranks it as important as task achievement:
     Disagree strongly 1 2 3 4 5 Agree strongly

Your score:

9–15 This seems to be a group, not a working team.
16–33 Teamwork is good: ask the team if they agree with your scores. Identify areas for improvement and work on them.
34–45 Ask the team if they agree with your scores. If they do, keep up the good work. Watch out for any slippage and react.

Figure 3.5 *Test your teamworking.*

SUMMARY

- Clarify your project organisation:
  – who is your project sponsor?
  – are all projects sponsored?
  – are all projects prioritised?
- Clarify and understand defined responsibilities of:
  – the project steering team;
  – the sponsor;
  – the project manager.
- Confirm your authority for the project.
- Recognise the importance of stakeholders.
- Focus on the dimensions of project leadership:
  – identifying and managing stakeholders;
  – managing the project dynamic lifecycle process;
  – managing performance of self, the team and the stakeholders.
- Select your core team carefully.
- Take positive actions to build the team:
  – regularly review performance;
  – test teamworking;
  – encourage participation;
  – celebrate and reward high performance.

Checklist 4 gives the key actions for effective leadership throughout the project.

CHECKLIST 4:
ACTIONS FOR EFFECTIVE LEADERSHIP

Throughout the project:

- Build trust and inspire good teamworking:
  - focus on behaviour and problems, not the person;
  - maintain self-esteem of others;
  - keep relationships constructive;
  - keep the team well informed at all times;
  - encourage ideas and suggestions;
  - involve them in decisions;
  - clearly define roles and responsibilities for all project tasks.

- Create a team identity:
  - clarify purpose and objectives;
  - confirm understanding and acceptance;
  - set clear personal targets;
  - recognise and praise effort;
  - celebrate team achievements.

- Encourage personal development;
  - assess individual abilities and experience;
  - assess training needs;
  - coach individuals to enhance skills;
  - appraise individual performance.

- Seek continuous improvement:
  - evaluate team processes and practices;
  - evaluate team performance;
  - encourage creativity and innovation;
  - devalue tradition and find better methods;
  - reward success.

- Resolve conflict and grievances promptly:
  - treat team members with respect;
  - encourage active participation;
  - listen to the team's views;
  - support problem-solving constructively.

- Champion and support the team:
  - help the team to reach consensus;
  - support team decisions;
  - look after their interests;
  - give guidance and assistance on request.

4

STARTING UP YOUR PROJECT

As you have seen earlier, projects are derived from many sources but it is important to establish a clear purpose that aligns to the strategic needs of the organisation. This does not preclude unforeseen opportunities being grasped to satisfy customer needs. Often the start-up of a new project is confusing and 'fuzzy' because you have:

- unclear direction;
- uncertainties about what is really required by everyone interested in the outcomes;
- confusion because people cannot stand back and take a holistic view;
- no clear idea about how to get some results;
- not been able to assess costs effectively;
- no clear idea of benefits which can be defined;
- no clear information on resources available;
- no clear idea about how long it will take.

You are enthusiastic and keen to dive in and get going and show some activity. It is prudent to review just what information you can now assemble to ensure the project does not set off in the wrong direction.

INFORMATION REVIEW

Who is your sponsor?

Are you clear who is sponsoring your project? It is most likely to be the person who gave you the project and informed you of your selection as the project manager. The sponsor, you will recall, is the person accountable for the project – that is the person held to account for a successful outcome. This may be your line manager or a manager or director one level higher in your organisation, but this is not always true.

Who is the customer?

Your next step is to identify who really is your customer and who is your main contact since you must start to build a working relationship with this individual. Many projects have multiple customers, even inside the organisation. Each customer has personal perceptions of what they want from your project and these perceptions will frequently generate hostility and conflict. You need to use all your skills of diplomacy to influence such a group and identify the needs and expectations of each customer.

One way to reduce the problems multiple customers create for you is to get them to agree that one of the group takes the role of *customer representative*. The customer representative is the key individual who has the necessary authority to take decisions affecting the project. Preferably this should not be a committee. For some larger strategic projects your organisation may prefer to appoint a *project board*. The purpose of such a group is to make sure that the departments who will be affected by the project and its outcomes are all represented as a collective customer. However, in such situations the chairperson of the project board is given the authority to act on behalf of the board when necessary.

Who will use the results?

Although the customer wants the results from the project, the customer is often not the person or group of people who will actually use the results on a day-to-day basis. You will need to have contact with the *end users* or a small representative group of the end users to check that you understand their needs and concerns about how the results will be used. With the assistance of the customer identify the end user representative who will be your future contact. Eventually you may decide to include this person in your project team. On larger projects a user group is appointed comprising four to six people.

The project core team

Up to now you may have found yourself working alone on the project. You must now collect together the core team for the project as soon as possible. This is the group of people who expect to work on the project for all or most of its life through to completion. Ideally you select the team members with the project sponsor and the line managers of the individuals identified as most likely to have relevant skills. They are probably going to come from the customer and the functional groups with an involvement in the project work.

Besides the core team you will require an extended team from time to time according to the amount of work. Regard these transitory team members as part of your team even though they may only be involved for a small period of time.

Checklist 3 gives you some questions to ask when selecting team members (see page 40). Try to be objective when you select your team. Remember your obligation is to select the right people for the project, not just whom you like!

CUSTOMER SATISFACTION

It is essential for you to recognise that customer expectations directly relate to customer satisfaction. Unfortunately there are degrees of satisfaction relating to the extent to which your customer perceives you understand their expectations and, what is more important, meet them with the results you have achieved. Fall short of these expectations and you will have unhappy customers.

Your goal is to have a delighted customer by providing all the expected results to an acceptable quality and standard. Fall short on the quality or performance standards expected and you will only create a complaining customer.

In addition the customer expects you to deliver on time – that is to an agreed schedule of delivery. This constitutes a promise by contract. Fail to deliver and you lose the respect of the customer and probably increase the project cost. This leaves you with a further issue of recovering the additional cost and a disgruntled customer is not too easy to convince they should accept the overspend.

Customers also expect you and eventually your project team to serve them with professional competence. You must ensure the right people with experience and appropriate skills are assigned to the project work, behave in a cooperative and friendly manner and demonstrate a real concern to meet the customer's expectations. This means everyone working on the project must understand the customer's environment and the difficulties and constraints they face. Do not add to the customer's problems – your job is to reduce them so always avoid announcing surprises. The customer wants you to provide positive results not a long list of excuses for poor performance and the problems of achieving results.

CUSTOMER NEEDS AND EXPECTATIONS

Defining the needs of the customer starts off a process that will ultimately allow you to produce deliverables specifically designed to meet the customer's expectations. Once you have established a clear understanding of the needs you can develop the requirements that drive the planning process.

Regard this as the preparation of the foundations of your project. Failure to give this activity appropriate time and effort will have continual impact on the project throughout its life. You can develop a superbly detailed plan but it never compensates for misunderstood needs or poorly specified requirements to satisfy those needs.

As a consequence the controls you initiate to keep the project on track will never yield data that interests your customer, because the plan is increasingly perceived as inadequate.

You must make a particular effort to:

- understand the customer – find out what makes them tick;
- understand the customer's environment in which they must operate;
- use political skills – not all customers are equal and some needs cannot be addressed for political reasons;
- demonstrate your technical competence and awareness of their technical needs;
- convert ill-defined needs into practical solutions;
- keep an open mind and a creative approach;
- analyse the mixed signals you receive through personal influences on needs;
- attempt to expose the hidden expectations.

Your purpose at this stage is to turn the information you receive into a clear statement of need that the customer can accept with no ambiguity.

Avoid the potential traps:

- Do not offer gold when silver is adequate – avoid striving for technical perfection beyond current capability or known state of the art. Simplicity is often more effective. Confirm that the customer understands the risks of going for leading edge solutions.

■ Effect of bias filters – it is easy for you to ignore needs for which you cannot think of an easy solution because it is outside your experience or knowledge.

Working with your customers can be frustrating. At times you will need to exercise all your communication skills to achieve a good, open relationship enabling the project to move ahead to achieve

CHECKLIST 5:
IDENTIFYING CUSTOMER NEEDS

Establish the current reality:

■ What happens now?
■ Is there an accepted process?
■ Are the process or procedures written down anywhere?
■ Who owns this process?
■ Is responsibility at each step clearly defined?
■ Is responsibility shared at any point in the process?
■ How do the process procedures interface with other processes?
■ Where are the decision points in the process?
■ Who has the authority to take decisions at each step in the process?
■ Why is a change necessary now?
■ What are the difficulties now that have promoted the need to change?

Identify needs and requirements:

■ What changes are identified:
■ Are these just a 'quick' fix or a quantum leap?
■ What does the customer believe is needed?
■ Do all customers agree?
■ Have the fundamental needs been separated from wishes?
■ Are predetermined solutions being proposed already?
■ Has the end user's perception of needs been identified?
■ Have the needs been listed as primary, secondary and hopes?
■ Has this list been prioritised and agreed with the customer?
■ Can you turn the information into clear 'statements of need'?
■ Can you use the needs analysis to derive a statement of requirements?
■ Does the customer agree with your statement of requirements?

the agreed objectives. Deriving the needs statements is a product of a partnership between you and your customer. This places an obligation on your customer to enter into the partnership with a serious intent to contribute openly and not sit on hidden agendas.

Try to persuade your customer to adopt a total lifecycle approach for the project, starting with needs and requirements through planning, execution, handover and full implementation. The project does not end with handover. You must check that the critical period after this phase is defined clearly for maintenance and service activities to ensure the customer agrees who is responsible.

THE CUSTOMER CONTRACT

You start to build a relationship with your customer through the establishment of needs and expectations. As project manager you have an obligation to turn this relationship into a form of contract. Often this is not a formal document signed by all parties but is an informal understanding. You may consider it appropriate to document some form of agreement on the obligations of yourself and the customer focused on achieving the desired outcomes.

Many projects acquire a reputation for poor management when the reality is poor customer performance in fulfilling their obligations. Success is only possible if everyone involved fulfils their responsibilities and the customer cannot claim it as their right to act in complete independence. You must meet the requirements of the schedule. This is only possible if the customer acts promptly when necessary in resolving issues and giving approvals. Delays and cost overruns occur too easily if customer response is slow. It suggests the customer is not so interested to get the results of the project on time.

IDENTIFYING THE PROJECT CONSTRAINTS

The constraints limit all project activities. In today's business environment it is rare for you to have unlimited resources, funding and time to complete the work. The project may yield significantly reduced benefits if you provide the results at a time when the requirements or the market needs have changed dramatically.

If you are intending to develop a new product, the date of availability to the sales team is critical to acquiring a significant market share and beating the competition. If the sales team cannot satisfy their customers and break promises, they risk losing important accounts. The organisation's credibility and reputation will suffer. It is always difficult to recover a frustrated customer and convince them such things will not happen again. It is known that a few months delay in getting a new product to the marketplace can lead to a huge reduction in the profit yield. The customers will buy a competitive product even if yours is better when it eventually arrives. You are then too late to grab a major share of the market without risking heavy advertising expenditure.

As we have discussed earlier, business needs are continually changing. Even with an internal project, late completion may lead others to conclude the whole effort was a waste of time because of new requirements. Project 'drift' sets in and you face what seems like a never ending project, trapped into acquiring a legacy of the 'project manager with the endless project'.

You must make sure as early as possible that all known constraints are identified. The customer will have decided how much they are prepared to pay for the project and this forces a cost constraint on the budget. Do remember that until you plan the project effectively no budget is accurate. Any budget set at this early stage is derived through inspiration or from historical comparative data.

Constraints usually fall into categories:

- *financial* – project cost, capital costs, materials, revenue and resource costs;
- *time* – time to deliver the results, the critical date when the results are needed;
- *quality* – the scope, specifications and standards to be achieved.

You need to explore each with your customer to gather the information you need to guarantee success. You will find that the customer will often be unable to answer your questions, arguing that it is part of the project work for you to uncover the answers.

THE KICK-OFF MEETING

Now that you have identified the key people with a close interest in your project, ask them to attend a kick-off meeting. The purpose is for you to understand what they expect from the project and allow them to confirm that you have a clear picture of the results they require at completion.

The project sponsor should chair and open the meeting to explain the strategic context of the proposed project. Explain why the project is important now and how it is prioritised in contrast to other active projects. Your purpose is to gain as much information as possible at this stage by asking questions. If you are fortunate the customer will have prepared a briefing document to initiate the project. However, validate the contents at this meeting to check you have a clear understanding of the requirements.

PROJECT KICK-OFF MEETING

Project: PRISM
Venue: Meeting Room 4   **Start time:** 10.30
Date: 5 May 1996   **Finish time:** 12.30

Purpose: Project inception meeting to establish relevant information for project definition

AGENDA
1. Introduction
2. Project background and assumptions
3. Project context
4. Project approach and strategy
5. Project objectives
6. Identification of constraints
7. Communication
8. Action points

Attendees:

John Foster	Sponsor (Chair)
David Johnson	Customer
Alison Williams	Customer
Angela Kimball	Customer
Alex Wimborne	End user representative
Anthony Barret	Project manager
Jane Foxbury	Team member
Jim Fawcett	Team member
Alan Davidson	Team member
Amanda Hunt	Team member

Please confirm your attendance.

Figure 4.1 *Kick-off meeting example agenda.*

Issue an agenda before the meeting to give attendees time to prepare. The customer and end user may bring two or three people to the meeting, but it is better to keep the group size down to a minimum where possible. Look at the example agenda format in Figure 4.1. Note the agenda does not include 'any other business' because this can frequently lead to open-ended discussion, diversion and ultimately loss of control of the meeting.

This meeting is the first time you collect together the team with your stakeholders. It is an opportunity for you to demonstrate your ability to lead the project team. Good preparation is important to achieve the meeting purpose.

CHECKLIST 6: PROJECT KICK-OFF MEETING

Background:

- Why is the project necessary?
- What is the overall problem or opportunity being addressed?
- Has the current situation been explored and understood?
- Has a statement of requirements been derived from the needs list?
- Is this an old problem?
- How long has it existed?
- Who wants to change things?
- Have previous attempts (projects) been made to address this problem?
- What information exists about past attempts to fix things?
- What assumptions have been made?

Context:

- Is the project in line with current organisational strategy?
- Does this project form part of a programme of projects?
- Will the project form part of a chain of linked projects or a programme?
- What is the timescale of the project?
- Is there a business critical date to get the results?
- Will the results be of value to another customer or part of the organisation?

Approach:

- Have all the needs been identified and analysed?
- Has a statement of requirements been agreed?
- Are there predetermined solutions?

- What are these solutions?
- Is there a best option and a least worst option?
- Is there enough time to explore more than one option?
- Are there known checkpoints for project review?
- What specialised skills are expected to be required for the project work?

Objectives:

- Are the project primary deliverables known?
- What does the customer need, want and wish to get from the project?
- Can these deliverables be clearly defined and specified?
- Does the end user agree with these deliverables?
- What does the end user need, want and wish to get from the project?
- What are the perceived project benefits?
- Have these benefits been quantified?
- Has a project budget been fixed?
- Is capital investment necessary?
- Has a capital expenditure request been initiated?
- Is time used for project work to be measured and costed?
- How were the costs derived?
- Has a cost/benefit analysis been carried out?
- Has a financial appraisal been carried out to establish payback?

Constraints:

- Have the project constraints been identified?
- Is there a time constraint for all or part of the deliverables list?
- Are there any financial constraints, eg manufacture cost, project cost?
- Is there a financial payback constraint?
- Are there any known technical constraints, eg new or untried technology?
- Are there known resource constraints?
- Is the project team to be located together on one site?
- Is part of the work to be carried out at another site?
- Is part of the work to be carried out by subcontractors or suppliers?
- Is there a preferred list of approved subcontractors and suppliers?
- What existing specifications and standards are to be applied to the project?
- Are there any legal constraints that might affect the project work?
- Are there any security implications?
- Are there any operational constraints, eg access to production areas/test equipment, etc?
- Are there any health and safety constraints?

PROJECT DOCUMENTATION

You are not alone – no one likes having to record information in a regular and organised manner. Project work produces a large amount of data and it is important that you record essential material. One of the greatest timewasters in project work is repeating the recording of information in different formats and the problems created in its interpretation later.

Start off your project by avoiding the 'I'll do it my way' syndrome. Insist that the team keep all essential project records on a standard set of templates derived specifically for the purpose. Throughout this book at the appropriate times you are given examples of standard templates. Some are more important than others and it is your decision which to use. This ensures everyone involved with the project records data in a consistent and disciplined manner without reinventing forms every week. In addition you get the right information recorded (and in the appropriate volume) for the project file to support your control system and aid project evaluation at completion. Expect an adverse reaction from people when you suggest using standard templates. It is viewed as 'form-filling' and a chore. Stress the importance of keeping everyone informed about what has happened in the project and that it is in their interests to get into the habit of keeping accurate records. Nobody can carry all the plans and information in their head!

All the templates suggested can be designed on a computer and networked for ease of completion from blank masters.

The first of these standard templates is the *project organisation chart* shown in Figure 4.2. It lists all those involved with the project, their line manager, location and telephone number. This is an important communication document for information and records agreed commitments of individuals assigned to the project team. Review the document regularly and keep it up to date. Set up a distribution list now identifying who gets which documents. Distribute copies to all those who need to know – both participants and non-participants.

The project file

Set up a project file for all the documentation related to the project. This file is the permanent record of the project and requires a disciplined approach to administration. Although you may prefer to use a paper-based system, some of your team may like to keep

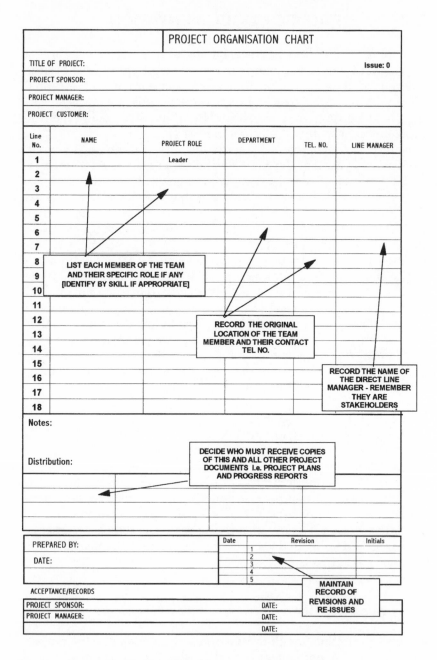

Figure 4.2 *A project organisation chart.*

all their records on a computer-based file or folder. This makes the distribution of information easier if you have a network. It also makes access and retrieval relatively easy. However, there is a potential difficulty with using the computer to store all the project data. If you cannot restrict access to your data, people can make changes without informing you and create confusion. Take precautions to prevent unauthorised access or modification of project documents and inform the team of their limits on the system. If you have concerns about reliability, always keep a hard copy of the project file – you cannot always take a computer into meetings off-site!

Organise your project file into sections for the different stages of the project, for example:

- Background information
- Project definition:
  - project organisation
  - stakeholders
  - project brief
- Project plans and schedules:
  - project risk management
  - responsibility charts
  - schedules
  - work plans
- Project execution and implementation:
  - project status reports
  - changes to project plans
  - action plans for corrective action
  - cost control data
  - supplier and subcontractor data
  - records of meetings
- Project closure:
  - handover checklist
  - acceptance process
  - follow-on and post-project responsibilities
  - project evaluation data
  - completion report

Divide into more detail if necessary. You are responsible for updating the file at regular intervals and it is a good habit to do this once a week. Always let others know where to find the file – it is most frustrating to search for a file that is hidden away!

The project log book

It is a good discipline to open a project log book at the start of your project. The purpose is to provide you with somewhere to record all events, agreed actions and forward planning ideas. The book is an A4 bound, lined book and *not* a loose-leaf file or folder. Record events with essential relevant data such as:

- date;
- time;
- who is involved;
- key points or content.

Events to record include:

- telephone calls – incoming and outgoing;
- faxes – incoming and outgoing;
- letters – sent and received;
- memos – sent and received;
- e-mail – sent and received;
- purchase instructions issued;
- contracts signed;
- action plans agreed;
- problems encountered;
- solutions derived;
- decisions taken – and how implemented;
- reports issued;
- meetings – sponsor, team, third party, one-to-one.

The log book is *not* a personal document – it is an addendum to the project file. When using a log book:

- use every page and number them sequentially;
- *never* remove any pages;
- start each day with a new page;
- *always* write in pen, ball-point or felt tip, *never* pencil;
- write on every line;
- rule out all unused lines at the end of each day and sign the page at the bottom;
- do not allow anyone else to write in the log book – even the project sponsor.

The log book is particularly valuable to record events with third parties like suppliers and contractors. When conflict and differences occur the log book provides a record of events that often takes the heat out of an argument. The record can have a legal status if a dispute eventually ends up in the hands of the legal profession!

The log book is an invaluable record of what actually happened through-out the project. It is useful for post-project evaluation and a source of archive data for other projects in the future.

THE PROJECT BRIEF AND SPECIFICATION

The kick-off meeting you have just completed will have been the focal point of all the initial work associated with the project start-up. The purpose of that meeting was to enable you and your team to understand the expectations of your customer and agree the requirements derived in the statement of requirements. The data you collect is enough for you to draw up a preliminary statement of the project objectives and the associated specifications.

This step is often the most difficult because you must now formulate in realistic terms just what the project is about and has to achieve. This is the foundation of project definition that we will examine in more detail in Chapter 5.

The *project brief* is a document that summarises all the relevant facts about the project and is therefore a source of definitive information. The contents include:

- the project origins – a need or opportunity statement;
- the project rationale – why is it necessary now?
- the benefits of the project – to the customer and your organisation;
- the project budget if known at this stage;
- the current timescale and deadlines – subject always to detailed planning later.

This document is ideally just one piece of paper, but for larger projects it often takes the form of a report with many different sections. Prefer the former as it forces you and the team to focus on real facts and not hopes or wishes. Unfortunately during the start-up of most projects there is too much expression of hopes and the 'wish list'. You have to resolve this conflict to sort out what you can achieve in practice with current technology, experience and knowledge compatible with the statement of requirements.

The project specification is a term applied to many different types of document and can include almost anything. Here the term specification describes any document that is an obligatory statement of procedures or processes that apply to the project. It is a statement of policy for the project.

These specifications can range from technical descriptions to quality standards or even organisational policy documents such as contract purchasing guidelines. When you come to define your project you will collect all the relevant specifications together in the project *scope of work statement*. This document is often referred to as the SOW and directly relates to your project brief to support the factual information included for approval by your customer.

SUMMARY

The key steps in project start-up are summarised in the flow diagram given in Figure 4.3.

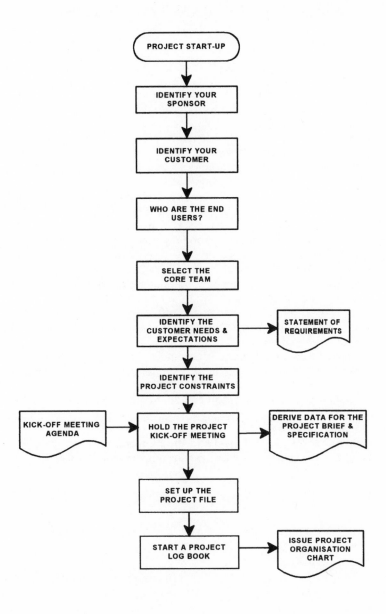

Figure 4. 3 *Process flow diagram — Project start-up.*

CHECKLIST 7: LEADERSHIP ACTIONS DURING PROJECT START-UP

- Identify your project sponsor.
- Identify your customer.
- Identify the end users of the project outcomes.
- Start to build a relationship with these people.
- Determine the project constraints.
- Agree a date for a kick-off meeting.
- Select your core team, then:
  - Hold an initial team meeting.
  - Explain the project background and context.
  - Explain the overall objectives of the project as you know them at present.
  - Confirm the team's understanding of the objectives.
  - Share your own enthusiasm and commitment to the project.
  - Listen to what the team members have to say.
  - Answer their questions if you can.
  - Promise answers to questions you cannot answer now.
  - Explain the project phases and the process you intend to use.
  - Empathise with their concerns about other commitments.
  - Explain your intention to have separate one-to-one meetings with each team member.
  - Agree dates for the first of these meetings.
  - Set up an initial programme of team meetings, say for the next four weeks.
  - Explain the kick-off process and confirm their attendance at this meeting.
- Open the project file.
- Prepare for the kick-off meeting with the team.
- Hold the kick-off meeting and record outcomes in the file.

5

DEFINING YOUR PROJECT

Now that you have completed the start-up process you have collected together all or most of the data needed to define your project and start the real journey towards success. You may ask at this point: 'What is the difference between start-up and definition?' The first is a data-gathering activity. The definition is the process of turning the data into something more solid and realistic, something that is no longer just a wish or a hope.

If you decide to build your house on some land already bought, you start by establishing the ground conditions. You then design the building, decide the type of materials you are going to use and the overall size and layout of the property. This process of gathering data enables you to design the appropriate foundations to support the building safely. It often takes longer than the actual building operation. The designs you derive are then submitted to statutory authorities to ensure they satisfy various mandatory regulations. Failure to provide your house with adequate and firm, well-defined foundations approved by the authorities will inevitably lead to structural failure of the building and incur possible legal or other consequences – the building may collapse!

The same is true for your project. You have spent a considerable amount of time and effort to gather all the relevant data in the start-up process to design the foundations of your project. The project brief is the summary document that contains the foundation design for your project. It is supported by numerous other documents as appropriate to the project.

Failure to give adequate time to this activity and derive all the relevant data for these foundations will lead to a poorly defined project with considerably reduced chance of achieving a successful outcome. The consequence of poor definition of the foundations is a project plan that is derived from incorrect or even misleading information. Like the building that collapses on poor foundations, your plan will soon start to fail and be discarded as a useless document. Your project goes out of control and you may suffer further serious consequences and criticism.

A clear definition of your project is critical to success – a large number of projects (more than 75 per cent) are perceived to fail as a consequence of poor or unclear definition.

WHAT IS NECESSARY TO DEFINE A PROJECT?

Five essential documents are required to define a project effectively:

- a statement of requirements;
- a stakeholder list;
- a project brief;
- a scope of work statement;
- a risk assessment.

All of these documents must be approved before you start the planning process. You are effectively returning the project definition to your customer saying:

> We have listened to you and understood what you need and require. We have examined these requirements and concluded what we believe we can realistically deliver to satisfy these needs. Now we are telling you what we understand we are going to provide for you with this project. Please approve these definition documents as they are the basis on which we will derive a plan and schedule for you to approve later.

The approval or 'sign-off' process is essential to maintain customer and project sponsor commitment to your project.

THE STAKEHOLDER LIST

When you start the definition process, the first step is to ask a simple question:

> Who has an interest in this project, now or in the future?

Some of these people you have already identified as key stakeholders:

- the customer;
- the end users;
- the project sponsor;
- the line managers of your core team members.

With your team you must now try to identify who has now or potentially will have in the future an interest. Consider that this could include:

- finance department;
- sales and marketing department;
- consultants;
- contractors;
- suppliers;
- other divisions or sites;
- the public;
- other agencies/statutory bodies.

In some projects where your customer is internal, there may be another party in the supply chain such as an end client with users.

All of these people have an interest that means they have an agenda of their own for the project. Although the controlling interest may be perceived as that of your customer, you cannot afford to ignore all others with an interest. They may consider their level of interest is enough to justify them having a voice to which you must listen. Failure to do so at this stage may lead to conflict, disruption and interference later. This group of people are the project stakeholders – all have strong feelings about their stake in the project and will make these feelings known to you probably when you least expect it!

Derive a complete list of the stakeholders as you now see them and record them on the *project stakeholder list*. A typical template is shown in Figure 5.1. This is not a single activity. Regularly update the list and reissue it. This is a communication document to keep everyone informed who has an interest in the project. But why, you ask, is this really so important? So far you have concentrated on the customer and the project sponsor for inputs to the project definition. As you saw in Chapter 4 all stakeholders need to be consulted for their inputs to give you a wider perspective of:

- the real project needs and requirements;
- what is realistically achievable in the timescale demanded.

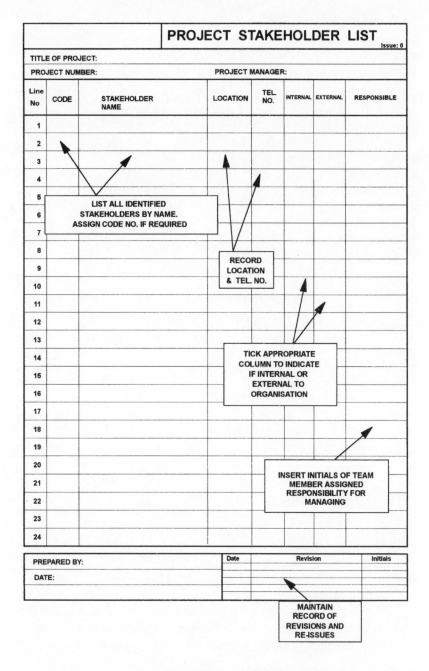

Figure 5.1 *Project stakeholder list.*

You use these additional data inputs in your work of defining the project. At this stage of the project you may not identify all the stakeholders, so review the list at each team meeting or project progress meeting, adding any newcomers as identified.

THE PROJECT BRIEF

From the kick-off meeting you held earlier you have derived most of the data for this document. Now you must ensure there is no amendment necessary as a result of consulting with any other stakeholders you have identified. A suggested template for a typical one-page document is shown in Figure 5.2. This contains a number of sub-headings:

- *Project title*. Give your project a relevant title for identification purposes. If appropriate also identify the project number if one has been assigned for financial budgetary control purposes.
- *Project overall objective*. It is appropriate to write an overall objective statement of about 25–30 words that describe the project desired results.
- *Project leader and project sponsor*. Identify yourself as the project leader and identify the project sponsor.
- *Project proposed start date*. This is the date when the real work starts after the definition is approved. This may not be the day of approval due to availability of the team and yourself. State a date when you expect to start planning if the project definition is accepted and the project approved to go ahead.
- *Project required end date*. State the date when the project is required to end with handover to the customer. This should be clear to you from the kick-off meeting, particularly if it is a business critical date for strategic reasons. This may be subject to change after planning is completed.
- *Project deliverables*. Identify the primary deliverables that will be seen from the project through its lifecycle. These are tangible outputs from the project which must be capable of being measured. Apply the SMART test to ensure each deliverable is:
  - *Specific* – clearly defined with completion criteria;
  - *Measurable* – understood metrics are available to identify delivery;
  - *Achievable* – within the current environment and skills available;

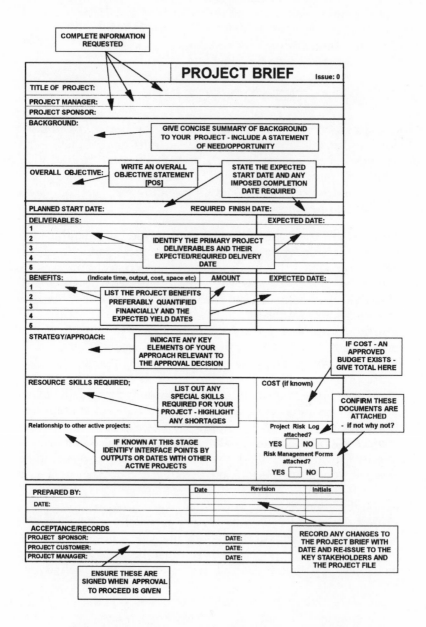

Figure 5.2 *An example of a project brief document.*

- *Realistic* – not trying to get the impossible with many unknowns;
- *Timebound* – is limited by a delivery date based on real need.

At this stage only five key deliverables are required, although after planning many more intermediate deliverables may be apparent.

- **Project benefits**. List what benefits you have identified for your organisation from the earlier investigative work you have completed. Try to quantify benefits, preferably measurable in financial terms – cost savings, increased turnover, contribution or profitability in a specific timescale. If in doubt apply the SMART test to benefits.

- **Project strategy**. State if you intend to examine more than one route to success, explore alternatives, carry out a feasibility study, set up a cross-site team, involve the customer in the team or anything else relevant to your approach to the project.

- **Project skills required**. Identify the skills required for the project work, highlighting particularly special experience and technical skills you expect to need. If necessary indicate if certain skills and expertise will be purchased from outside the organisation.

- **Relationship with other active projects**. Most organisations have many projects active simultaneously. Does your project interface at some point with another, either depending on it for inputs or providing outputs to another project? There are certain to be some critical interface dates which are mandatory for your project. Failure to recognise these interfaces can lead to both projects failing to meet completion on time.

- **Project cost**. If the cost is known or a budget exists from earlier studies or feasibility work then state the cost. If not, either give an estimated cost or leave blank until planning is complete. The relevance of cost depends on whether time is measured and costed or whether only capital expenditure is to be recorded here.

- **Risk management**. You are asked to indicate if the project risk log and risk management forms are attached to the document for approval. (See later in this chapter.)

In this document you have collected together all the known relevant facts upon which to base a decision to proceed. It is supported by another key document which contains the detailed specifications.

THE SCOPE OF WORK STATEMENT

As the name implies it is a narrative description of the project objectives in more detail, giving more information about each deliverable and benefit identified. What is more important the document (known as the SOW) must identify the boundary limits of the project, clearly stating what is *not* going to be done as part of the project.

The SOW is also a very convenient place for you to record all the constraints identified earlier and any assumptions made either during or after the kick-off meeting. These assumptions may have profound implications later during the project work.

The SOW is where the applicable specification list is recorded:

- internal product specifications;
- external product specifications;
- mandatory standards imposed by legislation;
- process specifications;
- customer specifications;
- standard operating procedures;
- purchasing procedures;
- quality standards;
- testing specifications and procedures;
- subcontract terms and conditions imposed on third parties.

Your purpose is to make sure that everyone knows from the outset which standards and specifications apply to your project. The document also identifies:

- where the actual documents can be found for reference;
- what exceptions, if any, apply to any specification for your project.

If necessary you can also use the SOW to record for reference purposes any other relevant documents that have been issued previously relating to the project, for example:

- cost-benefit analysis studies
- feasibility reports
- studies carried out by consultants
- project evaluation reports from previous projects

In practice similar projects often generate similar SOW statements so this is an opportunity for you to create a standard template. This is not a form this time, it is a detailed document that is kept as a master document. For each subsequent project the master need only then be edited and amended as appropriate for any project.

RISK MANAGEMENT

There are risks to all projects and *risk management* is the process of identifying and containing them to ensure your project's success. What is a risk?

A risk is any event that could prevent the project realising the expectations of the stakeholders as stated in the agreed project brief or agreed definition. A risk that becomes a reality is treated as an issue.

At the definition phase of a project it is valid for an initial risk assessment to be conducted. It might save you much wasted effort chasing an impossibly risky outcome and divert effort towards more beneficial projects with lower risks. Two fundamental types of risks are always present:

- *project risks* – associated with the technical aspects of the work to achieve the required outcomes;
- *process risks* – associated with the project process, procedures, tools and techniques employed, the controls put in place, communication, and stakeholder and team performance.

As project manager it is your obligation working with your team to:

- identify and evaluate potential risks;
- obtain agreement to action plans to contain the risks;
- take the actions and monitor the results;
- promptly resolve any issues arising from risks that happen.

There are two primary components of the process – assessment and monitoring. If you are only conducting a feasibility study at this stage, then each option must be examined for risk as the results could influence subsequent decisions.

Why is it necessary?

Once you have developed a realistic project schedule and detailed plan the project progress is measured against this plan. This schedule is your road map to success and anything that interferes with the progress will seriously damage your chances of success. Unfortunately even with the best prepared plan things can and will go wrong from time to time. These problems affect the

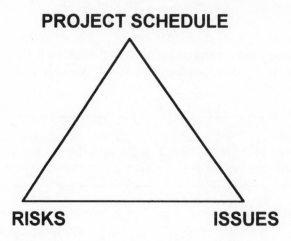

PROJECT SCHEDULE

RISKS

ISSUES

Figure 5.3 *Risks and issues impact on the project schedule.*

schedule leading you to recovery planning to overcome the problem and recover any time lost in the problem-solving process. Many of these problems can be anticipated in advance. How many times have you heard someone say, 'I could have told you this was going to happen'. You probably feel like taking some violent action when you hear such comments, no doubt because they contain a ring of truth! Use hindsight to question your own foresight in such situations. Could you have anticipated the problem? This is why it is necessary to carry out risk assessment – to anticipate what might go wrong and take action sometimes to avoid the problem.

The risks that happen become the issues that you must promptly resolve to maintain the integrity of the project schedule (see Figure 5.3).

There is always the possibility of unforeseen risks leading to unexpected issues. Provided you are prepared to react promptly you can still take the necessary actions to hold on to schedule dates. Identify the signals or triggers that suggest a risk is likely to happen and keep the team always alert to the possibility of any risk becoming a reality.

When is it necessary?

Risk management is a continuous process throughout the lifecycle of the project and you must maintain awareness of risk in the minds of all your project team:

- it should be started at the definition phase;
- it is essential to establishing the project brief;
- compile a complete list as a *project risk log*;
- review the list at regular intervals as the project moves forward.

Review the project risk log at regular intervals, normally monthly at project progress meetings unless decided otherwise by the project sponsor at the start of the project. You need to focus this review on:

- any change in the potential impact or probability of identified risks;
- any new high risks upgraded from a previously lower ranking are then subjected to closer examination;
- deriving contingency plans for either avoidance or damage limitation;
- adding any new risks identified to the list and assessing these for impact and probability.

Any risk entered on the list is *never* removed even if the time zone when it could occur has passed.

The list of risks from any project is a source of valuable learning data for future projects and is a useful data source for deriving checklists.

RISK ASSESSMENT

Any project has risks at the outset because of the many unknown factors, some of which you will remove during the planning stage. The risk could be due to external or internal factors. In practice risks disappear and new risks appear as the project progresses, so regularly review potential risks.

Risk assessment requires answers to some key questions:

- What exactly is the risk and its parameters?
- How serious is it as a threat to the project?
- What could be done to minimise its impact on success?

Call your team together and hold a brainstorming session to identify as many potential risks as possible – think of anything that could go wrong and hinder the project progress. Having identified all the risks review the list making sure none are repeated, then record them on a project risk log. A typical example is shown in Figure 5.4. Then attempt to establish two characteristics for each risk:

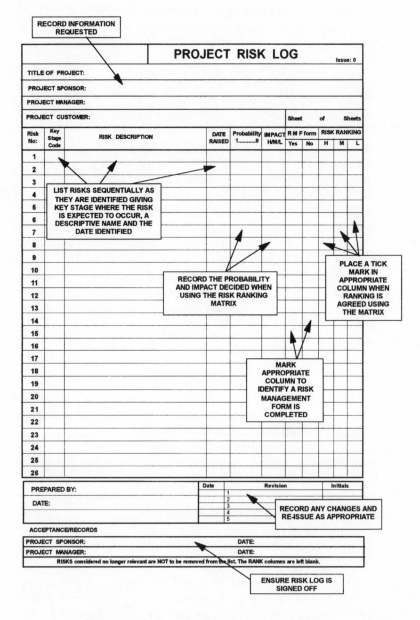

Figure 5.4 *An example of a project risk log.*

- What is the probability of it happening based on currently available data?
- What is the likely impact on the project if it does happen?

This assessment can only be subjective based on the previous experience of you and your team but you should attempt to reach a consensus for each risk identified.

Remember that *anything* that could go wrong and threaten the project is a potential risk and must not be ignored.

RANKING OF RISKS IDENTIFIED

.When you have derived your list of risks use the team's experience to decide for each risk:

- the probability of occurrence on a scale of 1 to 9:
    - 1 is low – most unlikely to happen;
    - 9 is high – very high probability it will happen;
- the impact on the project if it does happen;
    - *high* – significant effect on the schedule and project costs;
    - *medium* – less serious effect on the schedule, some effect on costs;
    - *low* – some effect on schedule, little effect on costs.

Remember this should be a team consensus decision using all the available information at the time. Generally there is a tendency to own-rate a risk by confidence that it can readily be dealt with if it

IMPACT ON THE PROJECT			
		LOW	MEDIUM	HIGH
PROBABILITY	**7 - 9**	*medium*	*high*	*unacceptable*
	4 - 6	*low*	*high*	*unacceptable*
	1 - 3	*low*	*medium*	*high*

Figure 5.5 *Risk ranking matrix.*

does happen. A word of caution though – it is better to up-rate a risk to ensure closer monitoring is carried out.

Once a set of risks has been assessed for impact and probability of occurrence you can rank them using a grid with the parameters of probability and impact on the project (see Figure 5.5). Each risk is located in the relevant box in the grid by the intersection of the impact and probability ratings assessed. Number each risk on your project risk log and use these numbers in the matrix to derive a ranking for the risk.

Risk current ranking

Assess the current ranking of all risks identified at the outset and subsequently during the project using the ranking matrix. Definitions are given below for high, medium and low rankings:

High	Major impact on the project schedule and costs. Serious consequent impact on other related projects. Likely to affect a project milestone. Must be monitored regularly and carefully.
Medium	Significant impact on the project with possible impact on other projects. Not expected to affect a project milestone. Review at each project meeting and assess ranking. Monitor regularly.
Low	Not expected to have any serious impact on the project. Review regularly for ranking and monitor.

Actions you must take

Any risks that clearly fall into a cell labelled 'unacceptable' must be closely analysed in more detail. If they could cause project failure decide if some changes to the project brief are necessary to reduce the level of risk. If you can do something now to reduce the ranking then you must derive and implement an action plan. No project should continue with such risks remaining (or a defined number of such risks). Derive and agree action or contingency plans to contain the possible damages. You may find it convenient to use a standard template for deriving these action plans. A typical template is shown in Figure 5.6 and the same format can be used to prepare contingency action plans for high risks.

If you decide to change the ranking of a risk at any time, record the change. If the change is too high then record the revised ranking on the project risk log and then reissue the document to the key stakeholders.

Checklist 8 gives you some typical questions to ask in risk assessment. Some of these are only applicable after the planning phase.

Risks change with time as the project work progresses, so review all risks and their ranking at regular intervals.

RISK MONITORING

Once risks to the project have been identified and action plans derived then these must be monitored to make sure prompt action is taken when appropriate.

Because any risk can change its characteristics with time, control of risk involves:

- allocating responsibilities for monitoring each risk identified;
- monitoring and reporting of actions agreed;
- monitoring of valid identified risks for any change of ranking.

We will consider this in the context of project control in Chapter 8.

Issues

An issue is a risk that has become a reality and needs to be resolved promptly. The relative importance of the issue and its impact dictates who will take corrective action. Some issues will need to be escalated for decisions to the project sponsor. Very serious issues are escalated to the senior management of the organisation.

You are responsible for ensuring that issues are dealt with promptly at the appropriate level and although you must monitor risks and outstanding unresolved issues, the project sponsor also has a part to play in the management of risks and issues.

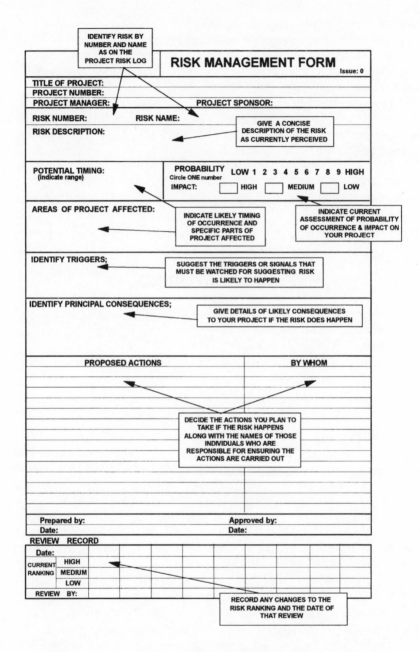

Figure 5.6 *An example of a risk management form for action planning.*

CHECKLIST 8: QUESTIONS FOR
RISK ASSESSMENT

YES   NO

❑	❑	Has the project leader's authority been established?
❑	❑	Is the core team appointed?
❑	❑	Does the core team understand the project purpose?
❑	❑	Have the project stakeholders been identified?
❑	❑	Have stakeholder management responsibilities been allocated?
❑	❑	Have the project objectives been established?
❑	❑	Have the project benefits been identified and quantified?
❑	❑	Are there clear deadlines and a project timescale?
❑	❑	Is there a known business critical date for completion?
❑	❑	Is there a scope of work statement?
❑	❑	Are the project boundary limits clearly established?
❑	❑	Is there an impact if the project fails?
❑	❑	Are the right skills available in the team/organisation?
❑	❑	Can the project brief be accurately derived?
❑	❑	Have all the project constraints been identified?
❑	❑	Are there identifiable consequences of late completion?
❑	❑	Has the project brief been approved?
❑	❑	Have all the key stages been clearly identified?
❑	❑	Have key stage dependencies been established and agreed?
❑	❑	Are the key stage durations agreed and accepted?
❑	❑	Is the project schedule realistic and achievable?
❑	❑	Have key stage responsibilities been allocated and accepted?
❑	❑	Are the resources realistically available?
❑	❑	Have workload priorities been clearly established?
❑	❑	Have line managers accepted and committed their staff involvement?
❑	❑	Have all resources required given commitment to their responsibilities?
❑	❑	Has the plan been developed to a low enough level for effective control?
❑	❑	Have key stakeholders signed off the project plans?
❑	❑	Are project procedures established and understood?
❑	❑	Has a milestone schedule been established?
❑	❑	Have performance measures been derived?

Any questions to which the answer is **NO** must be examined further to establish the consequences and, if significant, contingency action plans must be derived.

YES	NO	
❏	❏	Is there an impact of doing nothing?
❏	❏	Are staff/organisational changes possible/expected during the project?
❏	❏	Are business requirements likely to change during the project?
❏	❏	Is new technology involved?
❏	❏	Are new techniques to be employed?
❏	❏	Are new suppliers/contractors to be used?
❏	❏	Is the project dependent on another project?
❏	❏	Are there possible constraints on third parties?
❏	❏	Can third parties impose constraints on the project work?

Any questions to which the answer is **YES** must be examined further to establish the consequences and, if significant, contingency action plans must be derived.

GETTING YOUR PROJECT DEFINITION APPROVED

The final step in the definition process is to present your documented definition to the project sponsor and your customer for approval to go on to the planning phase. Before you take this final step check that you have done everything necessary to fully and clearly define the project – see Checklist 9.

Getting agreement and approval is often best carried out in a meeting to enable you to explain any decisions you have taken following the earlier kick-off meeting.

Approval of the project definition usually requires the following documents to be presented:

- the project organisation chart;
- the project stakeholder list;
- the scope of work statement;
- the project risk log;
- the risk management forms for 'high' risks;
- the project brief.

If the project is of a confidential nature then you must show how all project documentation is to be kept secure and that all documents display appropriate security classification codes.

It is good practice for the project sponsor to sign all documents as approved, acting on behalf of all stakeholders. The customer must, of course, indicate their acceptance of the project definition by also signing the project brief.

CHECKLIST 9:
DEVELOPING THE DEFINITION

Ask:

- Is the project organisation clearly established?
- Are roles and responsibilities at all levels understood and accepted?
- Are project accountability and authority statements issued?
- Has a project organisation chart been prepared and issued?
- Has the project stakeholder list been prepared and issued?
- Have all the key stakeholders been identified?
- Have stakeholder management responsibilities been allocated in the team?
- Has a project need/purpose/opportunity statement been agreed?
- Has all the relevant background information been collected?
- Is there an overall project objective statement agreed?
- Is the corporate and strategic context and priority of the project understood?
- Is the customer identified?
- Is a client project team involved?
- Are the project boundary limits clearly established?
- Is there a business critical date for the completion of the project?
- Are the project deliverables clearly identified?
- Have the project benefits been established?
- Has the project approach and strategy been agreed?
- Has a preliminary resource skill analysis been carried out?
- Is the project related to other projects?
- Is the impact on other projects understood?
- Have the project risks been identified and quantified so far?
- Has a project risk log been prepared?
- Have risk management forms been prepared for 'high' risks?
- Has a scope of work statement been prepared?
- Have all assumptions made so far been documented clearly?
- Are existing communication procedures acceptable for the project?
- Has a project brief been prepared ready for approval?

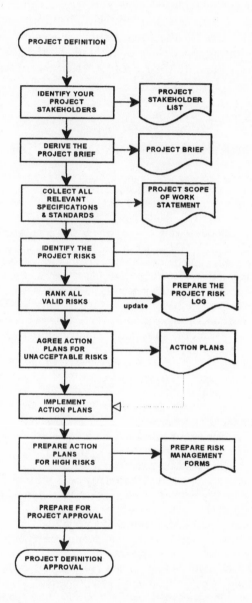

Figure 5.7 *Process flow diagram — project definition.*

SUMMARY

The key steps of project definition are shown as a flow diagram in Figure 5.7. Checklist 10 summarises the key leadership actions for the definition phase of the project.

CHECKLIST 10: KEY LEADERSHIP ACTIONS DURING PROJECT DEFINITION

■ *Project stakeholders*:
- – Confirm needs and expectations.
- – Confirm the statement of requirements.
- – Clarify the project purpose and context.
- – Establish authority and accountability.
- – Confirm project deadlines.
- – Confirm the project constraints.

■ *Project tasks*:
- – Confirm the key stakeholders.
- – Identify the project deliverables.
- – Identify the project benefits.
- – Decide the project strategy/approach.
- – Establish the project budget.

■ *Project team*:
- – Involve the team in project definition.
- – Hold regular team meetings.
- – Clarify the project objectives.
- – Encourage ideas and suggestions.
- – Listen to team views.
- – Involve in the decision process.

■ *Team members*:
- – Identify special training needs.
- – Hold regular one-to-one meetings with team members.
- – Encourage participation.
- – Reinforce motivation with responsibility.
- – Understand personal objectives.
- – Review skills and experience.
- – Resolve conflicts promptly.

PLANNING YOUR PROJECT

A successful project does not just happen, you have to do a host of things to make it happen. Having spent a considerable effort to get your project clearly defined it is now essential for you to plan the work in a logical and structured manner. Some of your colleagues may suggest you can just plan as you go along – try it and see how often you have to do rework and see your project go through cycles of stop–go–stop–go. Yes, you may eventually reach the end of the project, but at considerable cost to the organisation and your health! Consider the stress induced in your team members struggling to keep the work moving without any clear idea of when each piece of work should be completed or how it links into the next piece of work.

Planning is a process of creating order out of apparent chaos, made complex by the environment in which you are operating, where you continually face change. In its simplest approach, planning is just a process of asking questions:

- What actions need to be done?

  _____

  _____

  _____

  _____

- When are these actions to be done?

  _____

  _____

_____

_____

- Who is going to do them?

  ✎

  _____

  _____

  _____

- What equipment and tools are required?

  ✎

  _____

  _____

  _____

- What is not going to be done?

  ✎

  _____

  _____

  _____

The answers to these questions lead you to consequential questions but your purpose is to convert the contents of the project brief to a form that everyone understands. The objective for you and your team is to achieve the results on time, to the budgeted cost and to the desired level of quality. Project planning is carried out to:

- reduce risks and uncertainty to a minimum;
- establish standards of performance;
- provide a structured basis for executing the work;
- establish procedures for effective control of the work;
- obtain the required outcomes in the minimum time.

You are rarely confident enough to plan all the detailed work of your project at this stage. Too often the outputs from early work do not give expected results and you have to take this into account to plan the detail of the following work. If the plan is fully detailed you must spend time replanning and reworking the earlier planned detail. This difficulty is always with you but can be overcome to a large extent using the right tools and techniques. Planning is a dynamic and continuous process to enable you to remain proactive throughout the project. You only finish planning when you finally close the project file.

Who needs to be involved?

The short answer is you and your project core team together. Before you start your first planning session, review the skills and experience of the team members. If you can identify any short-comings in skills, knowledge or experience needed for planning, then seek to fill the gaps now by inviting other people to join your planning session. Invite experts from other departments to join you, stressing that this is not committing them to project work later and that you value their inputs to your efforts. Persuade your project sponsor to attend and open the planning session, explaining the project strategic context, relevance and priority. Planning is essentially a participative activity that motivates your team, contributes to team building and creates team 'buy-in' to the plans derived – this commitment is essential to success. Producing a plan yourself and then seeking agreement from everyone else is a long process that does not create a sense of commitment in your team. It becomes 'your plan' and not 'our plan'.

WHERE DOES PLANNING START?

This is always subject to debate and argument. The options are:

- top down – identifying the principal blocks of work involved;
- bottom up – identifying all the tasks to be carried out.

A third option – working backwards from the completion date – is often suggested but as this is subject to huge risks at this stage it is not recommended.

The top-down method suffers from the disadvantage that the blocks identified are likely to be based on functional activities that may only be few in number. This creates a significant loss of potential concurrency of the work – activities that can be carried out in parallel. As a result the blocks are arranged in series.

The bottom-up approach suffers from a disadvantage that it takes a long time to identify all the tasks to be carried out and a huge number can be identified. You are then faced with the difficulty of arranging them in the right sequence for optimum time in a project schedule. In addition you almost certainly forget or miss some tasks.

Before going any further, some terms have been introduced which need defining:

- *a task* – a (relatively) small piece of work carried out by one person;
- *an activity* – a parcel of work of the project comprising several tasks, each of which may be carried out by different people;
- *concurrent activities* – activities (or tasks) that are designed to be carried out in parallel, ie at the same time;
- *series activities* – activities (or tasks) that are designed to be carried out one after another, each strictly dependent on completion of the earlier activity.

As an example, producing a report is an activity but it comprises many tasks:

1. gathering data from different sources – in parallel;
2. analysing data;
3. writing first draft of report;
4. editing the draft;
5. preparing the graphics of charts and diagrams;
6. preparing the final draft – in parallel with 5;
7. introducing final copy for reproduction;
8. reproduction and issuing the report.

It may even be possible to break down some of these tasks into even more detail (or sub-tasks) if different people are involved in writing different sections of the report.

Successful planning is a mixture of both approaches to reduce the difficulties and arrive at a plan that has sufficient detail to maximise concurrency. You start by identifying the *key stages* of your project.

IDENTIFYING THE KEY STAGES

The essential process in planning is to use collective experience and knowledge of your project team and others invited to the planning session to identify the work as a list of tasks to be done.

This is carried out in a brainstorming session to derive a full list of tasks. Write everything down on a flip chart and when carrying out these sessions remember to follow the basic rules of:

- quantity before quality – even if the same tasks appear more than once;
- suspend all judgement – disallow any critical comments.

The list derived is not ordered or ranked with any priorities at this stage and may seem to be a complete jumble from which no sense will ever appear. When everyone feels they have run out of ideas for tasks you can suspend the brainstorming activity. There are now several flip chart sheets containing many tasks. The next task for the team is to reduce the long list, initially cleaning it up by removing obvious duplicates. Then start to cluster together those tasks that are clearly related together (as in our earlier example of the report) either in series or parallel. Aim to reduce your task list to a reasonable number of activities, preferably in the range 30–60 depending on the size of the project.

These are the key stages of your project from which everything else is developed. The forgotten tasks lose significance for the moment as they are hidden away in the key stages and you can return to the detail later. This approach generally helps you identify most of the possible concurrency now and gives you an activity list of a size that is relatively easy to manipulate. You may find that later you will split key stages into two or more to improve the accuracy of your plan. In practice your clustered list of activities will be at least 90 per cent accurate or frequently even better. Do not steamroller this step, it is the basis on which all subsequent planning is carried out, so spend time to save time later!

Using the key stages

Once the key stages are known and agreed you organise them into a logical sequence to maximise concurrency. There are some traps here for you:

- avoid considering real time or dates yet;

- avoid assigning people or functions to the key stages.

Both will lead you to create errors in the project logic. The next step is to derive the *project logic diagram*. This is done using a technique known as taskboarding. Write each key stage on a separate small card or self-adhesive notelet sheet. Use these as parts of the project 'jigsaw' to build the picture. Arrange them in the right logical order either on a table, using a whiteboard or simply use the office wall. This is achieved by taking each key stage in turn and asking:

What must be completed before I can start this work?

The first key stages should start from a card labelled 'Start'. Continue working from left to right until all the notelet sheets have been used. Connect all the notelets with arrows to show the logical flow of the project from start to finish.

The advantage of this technique is that everyone can be involved. The graphic impact of the diagram developing makes each member of the team question and debate the validity of the logic as it grows. An example of a logic diagram is shown in Figure 6.1.

Note that the logic diagram is continuous, ie every key stage has at least one arrow entering (an input) and at least one arrow leaving (an output). To assure integrity of the logic this rule must be maintained otherwise the plan will contain errors. Of course it is not unusual to find more than one arrow depicting dependency entering and leaving some key stages.

Note also that the basis of the logic is that a new activity cannot logically start until all immediate previous activities finish. If you find on reviewing the logic that a following task can start earlier than the end of the previous key stage, it must be split to show that earlier dependence. For example, from the logic diagram in Figure 6.1 the 'design phase 1' has been split into two to allow 'purchase orders' to start before the end of 'design phase 1' to give the result shown in Figure 6.2.

The basic rules for deriving the logic diagram are given in Checklist 11.

Though you have derived the diagram it is worth considering keeping a record of all the dependencies you have agreed. You may use this information to input to project management software later to prepare the schedule. When recording dependencies only record each immediate predecessor key stage number to any particular key stage.

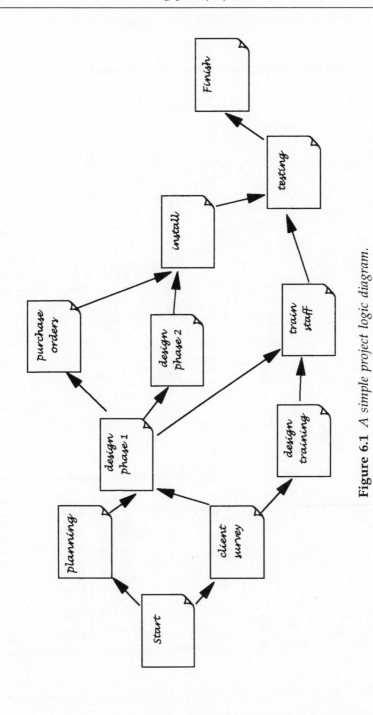

Figure 6.1 *A simple project logic diagram.*

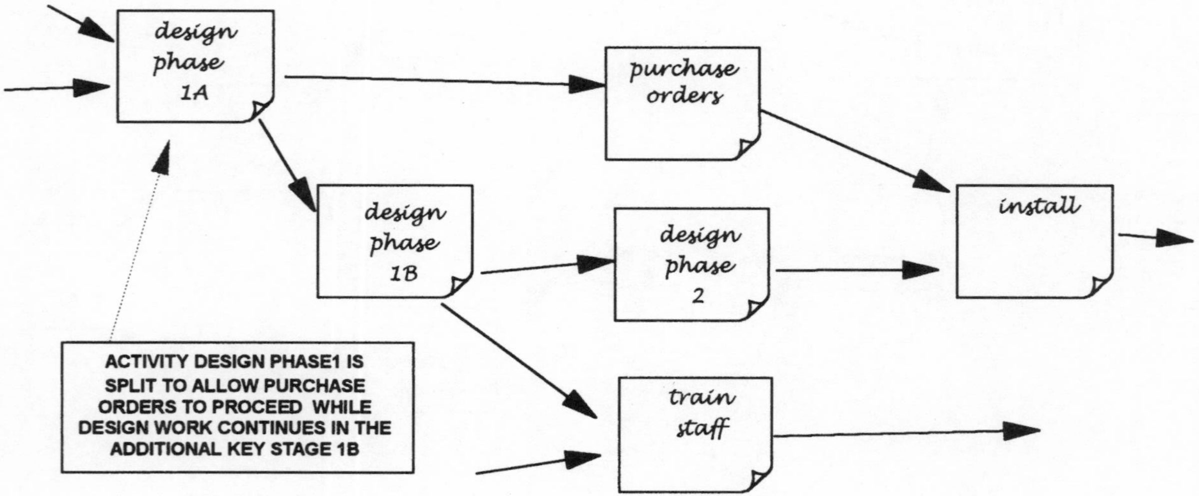
design phase 1A
purchase orders
design phase 1B
design phase 2
install
train staff
ACTIVITY DESIGN PHASE1 IS SPLIT TO ALLOW PURCHASE ORDERS TO PROCEED WHILE DESIGN WORK CONTINUES IN THE ADDITIONAL KEY STAGE 1B

Figure 6.2 *Splitting a key stage to improve project logic.*

CHECKLIST 11: DERIVING THE PROJECT LOGIC DIAGRAM

- Time flows from *left* to *right*.
- There is no timescale on the diagram.
- Place a 'Start' notelet at the extreme left of the sheet.
- Place a 'Finish' notelet at the extreme right of the sheet.
- Make sure you have prepared a separate notelet for each key stage.
- Start each KEY STAGE description with a verb (present tense).
- Do not attempt to add durations for the key stage yet.
- Use different colour notelets if appropriate for different functional activites.
- Locate the notelets on the sheet in order of dependency – debate each one.
- When all notelets are used up validate the dependencies – try working back.
- Show the dependency links as 'Finish' to 'Start' relationships initially.
- Do not take people doing the work into account – this can produce errors.
- Do not add in responsibilities at this stage.
- Draw in the dependency links with straight arrows in pencil.
- Avoid arrows crossing as it leads to confusion.
- Label each key stage with an alphanumeric code:
  AB, AC, AD, AE, etc.
  Do not use I or O to avoid confusion with one or zero.
- When satisfied it is correct *record the dependencies*.
- If appropriate tape the notelets down to the sheet then roll it up for filing.

THE PROJECT WORK BREAKDOWN STRUCTURE

The work breakdown structure (usually referred to as the WBS) is a convenient means of graphically presenting the work of the project in a readily understandable format. The use of a hierarchical form of structure is surely familiar to most people and is shown in Figure 6.3. It is easy to prepare, the project key stages forming the highest level of the WBS which is then used to show the detail at the lower levels of the project. You know that each key stage comprises many tasks identified at the start of planning and later

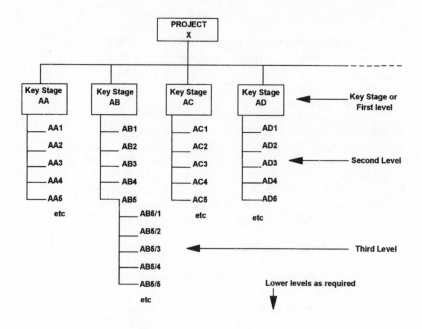

Figure 6.3 *The work breakdown structure.*

this list will have to be validated. Expanding the WBS to the lower levels is the process of multi-layer planning you will use throughout the project.

The WBS has many uses apart from just showing the work structure.

Note that:

■ The WBS does *not* show dependencies other than a grouping under the key stages.
■ It is not time based – there is no timescale on the drawing

---

The WBS is a dynamic tool which must be updated as the work proceeds, particularly as minor changes affect the task analysis.

Now that you have identified the key stages and the WBS for your project the next step is to insert some time estimates into the plan. However, there is one intermediate step that is worth considering at this stage.

ALLOCATING RESPONSIBILITY

Each of the key stages of the project needs to be owned by one of your team members. This allocation of responsibility is essential to make sure the work is done on time and your objective is to fairly and evenly distribute the work in the team. You must persuade each member of the team to accept the role of *key stage owner* for one or more key stages. Occasionally this may be a departmental representative who accepts responsibility for the work to be completed on time. This person is responsible within their department for the processes used to achieve the results desired.

The key stage owner (KSO) accepts the obligation for his or her key stage to confirm:

- the work required is identified at task level;
- the dependencies are clearly identified;
- the estimates of durations are accurate;
- the work gets done on time to the quality needed;
- the work conforms to quality assurance (QA) procedures and requirements;
- regular monitoring is maintained;
- regular accurate status reports are issued;
- problems and issues are alerted promptly to you.

Ensure your team members have:

- the necessary authority to get the work done;
- a strong sense of commitment to the project;
- the tools for the job;
- the essential environment for quality to be maintained;
- access to the right skills for the work;
- the visible support of both yourself and the project sponsor;
- a clear understanding of the performance expected of them.

Allocating responsibility is not a matter of random choice or an auction, you must heed the current circumstances of each individual. Some guidelines are given in Checklist 12.

Record your allocated responsibilities

Keep a record of the responsibilities you have allocated. This is a key communication document for everyone involved including the

---

CHECKLIST 12: SOME GUIDELINES FOR ALLOCATING OWNERSHIP

Consider:

- individual capabilities;
- depth of knowledge;
- previous relevant experience;
- the speed of working;
- the accuracy of past work;
- creative ability demonstrated previously;
- problem-solving ability;
- personal time management ability;
- personal development objectives;
- individual work style – team or loner?
- current workload – other projects;
- current functional workload;
- capacity to do the work on time;
- previous performance record;
- personality conflicts;
- who can provide advice, support and back-up;
- whether additional training is necessary now or in future.

Consider also whether:

- the tools and equipment are available;
- the essential technical skills exist;
- any special training is required.

---

line managers of the resources assigned to the project. As the plan develops more names are added as the extended team is identified for parts of the detailed work. A suggested format is shown in Figure 6.4.

This document lists out the key stages and the name of the individual responsible for the work involved in that key stage. Also you will note the template includes the name of the individual consulted for advice, who may be an expert in the organisation, not necessarily yourself. At this stage of planning you do not have the data to complete the 'Duration' or 'Plan End Date' columns. Issue the document to all those on the list and anyone else you consider needs to know.

Your reason for allocating these responsibilities is to assign the estimating of key stage durations to those people in your team who are most likely to have the appropriate experience.

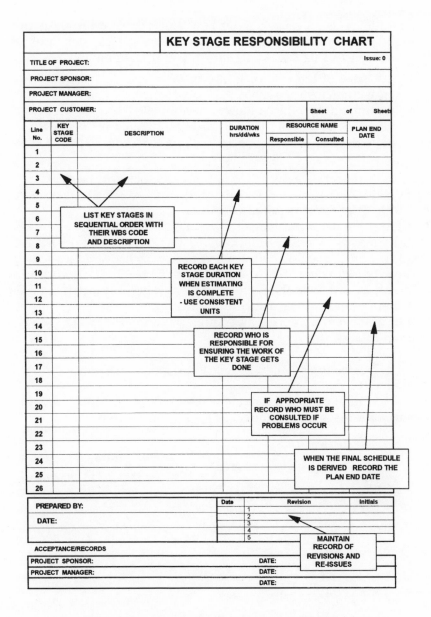

KEY STAGE RESPONSIBILITY CHART

Issue: 0

TITLE OF PROJECT:

PROJECT SPONSOR:

PROJECT MANAGER:

PROJECT CUSTOMER:

Sheet   of   Sheets

Line No.	KEY STAGE CODE	DESCRIPTION	DURATION hrs/dd/wks	RESOURCE NAME		PLAN END DATE
				Responsible	Consulted	
1						
2						
3						
4						
5						
6						
7						
8						
9						
10						
11						
12						
13						
14						
15						
16						
17						
18						
19						
20						
21						
22						
23						
24						
25						
26						

LIST KEY STAGES IN SEQUENTIAL ORDER WITH THEIR WBS CODE AND DESCRIPTION

RECORD EACH KEY STAGE DURATION WHEN ESTIMATING IS COMPLETE - USE CONSISTENT UNITS

RECORD WHO IS RESPONSIBLE FOR ENSURING THE WORK OF THE KEY STAGE GETS DONE

IF APPROPRIATE RECORD WHO MUST BE CONSULTED IF PROBLEMS OCCUR

WHEN THE FINAL SCHEDULE IS DERIVED RECORD THE PLAN END DATE

PREPARED BY:	Date	Revision	Initials
	1		
DATE:	2		
	3		
	4		
	5		

MAINTAIN RECORD OF REVISIONS AND RE-ISSUES

ACCEPTANCE/RECORDS

PROJECT SPONSOR:	DATE:
PROJECT MANAGER:	DATE:
	DATE:

Figure 6.4 *An example of a key stage responsibility chart.*

WHAT IS AN ESTIMATE?

An estimate is a decision about how much time and resource are required to carry out a piece of work to acceptable standards of performance. This therefore requires you to determine:

- the 'size' of the task or group of tasks – as determined from measurements if possible;
- the amount of 'effort' required to complete the work – how can the work be broken down? Can it be divided between two or more people? Effort is measured in project time units – hours/ days/weeks (see Figure 6.5).

Once the effort is known then optimise the resource needs, taking individual capacities or available time into account to determine the levels of effort required from each.

Effort is a direct measure of a person's time to do a piece of work in normal work days. Unfortunately that person will often have other non-project activities to complete which reduces their capacity to do the work. At a capacity of 50 per cent the work will take at least double the number of work days. In practice it takes longer because of the 'back-track' effect due to the breaks in the flow of the work. Effort is measurable as continuous work with no interruptions.

Duration is a conversion of effort taking into account the number of people involved, their capacities and an allowance for non-productive time.

Since duration is measured in real working days this is never the same as the schedule, which has to take into account:

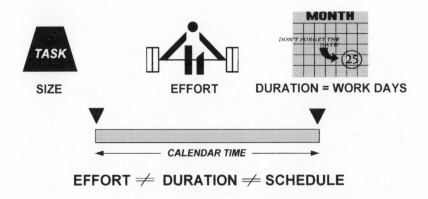

Figure 6.5 *Relationship between effort, duration and schedule.*

- non-available days for project work;
- non-working days – weekends;
- public and organisation holidays;
- staff holidays.

The first step for you is to derive some realistic durations and then apply these to a calendar to derive a schedule.

ESTIMATING THE DURATIONS

As the duration of each key stage is the real time it will take to complete the work this is usually the most difficult part of the planning process. Unfortunately there is an abundance of 'good advice' in most organisations about how long a piece of work will or should take. The process appears to be one of part art and part science that is hardly surprising since you are really trying to predict the future! So far no one has produced a reliable crystal ball!

The sources for accurate estimates are limited:

- experience of others;
- the expert view;
- historical data from other projects.

There is no substitute for experience. If similar work has been done before then you can ask others for their own previous experience and adjust the data for your project. It is a reasonable way to start but always take a cautious approach.

The data you collect this way will often hide important relevant information. No one will easily admit taking longer than the plan predicted for a piece of work – particularly if slippages caused problems. Also people's memories have a habit of only remembering the good news with the passage of time. If good plans and records exist review these to determine what actually happened compared to what was planned to happen. Take more than one opinion if you can and remember no two people ever do the same piece of work at the same pace. The equation relating effort and performance is different for us all.

Who are the experts? There may be a few – or so they believe! Always ask questions about how reality compared with original estimates for some work. Check that the nature or content of the work did not change. You soon discover who is above average at estimating accurately – the expert(s) you desperately seek. Since it is relatively rare for work to be identical between different projects then apply an adjusting factor to arrive at a duration for your activities. Keep a record of how you derived the estimates in case you are wrong, then you can improve your estimating skills.

People problems

Ask anyone how long a piece of work will take and you are likely to be given a shrug and a smile and a wildly inaccurate answer. This is because they do not ask themselves some simple questions:

- Do I really understand what is involved?
- Do I have all the necessary skills and tools for the work?
- What else must I do at the same time?
- What is the priority of the project work over other work?
- When is it really needed by?
- Can I break the job down into chunks to do at different times?
- Can I predict what I will be doing when this project work needs to be done?
- Will I be taking any holiday during the time concerned?
- Do I have any other obligatory commitments during the time concerned?
- What does my manager know about my future commitments that I do not know yet?

The reality is that the majority of people are not productive 100 per cent of the time! As much as 20 per cent of the working week is taken up by:

- meetings – particularly ones they need not attend;
- general interruptions:
  - visits to their desk and to others – wanderlust!
  - equipment failure;
  - reading journals and e-mail;
  - searching for information;
  - giving support and advice to others;
- commitments to routine functional work and other projects;
- unforeseen events;
- seeking advice from others;
- communication failures;
- personal organisation;
- engaging in conflict;
- inability to say 'no' to others' requests.

Consider also:

■ project complexity:
  – specifications – adequacy, unfamiliarity;
  – new quality standards;
  – unclear understanding of the technology;
  – new technology – always has a learning curve for confidence;
■ team size and location of the team members;
■ anything else you can think of!

The answers to these and other similar questions are often ignored in deriving an initial estimate, leading to considerable problems later. Rash promises are assumed as realistic and inserted into the plan.

CONTINGENCIES

The purpose of contingencies is to attempt to quantify the extent of uncertainty in the estimating process that make up the project plans.

Contingencies are not intended to cover changes to the project definition or objectives after they have been agreed with the stakeholders.

If such changes occur then the contingencies are rolled forward and adjusted. Ask:

■ What factor can you use for adjusting people's estimates?
■ Is that factor global for all estimates or different for different types of work and for different people?
■ Should you expose your adjustment factor(s)?
■ What limits must you use in applying contingency?
■ Should you multiply some estimates by an additional weighting for:
  – team size?
  – team experience (in individuals)?
  – team working history of this team?
  – project complexity?
  – project use of new techniques or technology?
  If so, what should it be?

You take the final decision what figures for 'durations' you intend to insert into your plan. These lead you to calculating the total project time with a projected completion date. Obviously there is a balance between the desired project completion date and the projected or forecast completion date based only on estimates. The former may well appear to be almost impossible and quite unrealistic, the latter insupportable and good justification for cancelling the project! Somewhere in the middle there is an acceptable solution and only attention to detail and all the experience you can gather will help you to find it.

TIME LIMITED SCHEDULING AND ESTIMATES

There is always a conflict when a completion date is imposed on a project before any work on estimates is carried out. This imposed date is outside your control completely so you then attempt to compress estimates to fit the plan. To a limited degree this is acceptable as a target but too often this process moves you into a totally unreal situation where you are faced with 'Mission Impossible'. You must still prepare realistic estimates to derive a clear case and state:

- what you can deliver in the time;
- what you cannot deliver in the time;
- why you can only meet part of the objectives of the project.

You can then use your skill as a negotiator to arrive at an agreed solution!

Since the major portion of all project costs is frequently the time expended, the accuracy of estimates is a key factor in achieving project success. Historical data can be valuable even from parts of previous projects as an initial guide. Analysis of the actual proposed work is essential if accurate estimates are to be derived. Even then people seem to habitually underestimate time for the execution of work. There are some people who have an intuitive ability to visualise the work involved and give accurate estimates – identify and make good use of them!

Some practical guidelines that can be used are:

- Schedule full-time team members at 3.5–4.0 working (productive) days per week (to allow for holidays, absences, training courses, etc).
- Include management time where appropriate as an additional 10 per cent.

- In planning, avoid splitting tasks between individuals.
- When tasks are split between two individuals do not reduce time by 50 per cent – allow time for communication and coordination.
- Take individual experience and ability into account.
- Allow time for cross-functional data transfer and responses.
- Build in time for unscheduled urgent tasks arising on other non-project activities.
- Build in spare time for problem-solving and project meetings.
- Include appropriate contingencies at *all* levels of planning.

Any estimate is only as good as the data upon which it is based so, like project risks, accept they may change with time as more data becomes available to you. As the project continues always review and validate the durations you have used. For each key stage keep a record of:

- the estimates you have decided finally;
- any assumptions made during estimating;
- where contingencies have been added;
- how much contingency has been added.

Now with durations agreed you can analyse the logic diagram for its critical path.

IDENTIFYING THE CRITICAL PATH OF YOUR PROJECT

Critical path techniques have been in use on projects now for some 30 years, having proved their value as a tool for project scheduling and control. The fundamental purpose is to enable you to find the shortest possible time in which to complete your project. You can do this by inspection of the logic diagram.

Enter the durations onto your notelets in the logic diagram for each key stage. Begin at the 'Start' notelet and trace each possible route or path through the diagram to the 'Finish' notelet, adding the durations of all the key stages in the path. The path that has the highest number, ie the longest duration, is the *critical path* of your project and is the shortest time to complete the project. All other paths are shorter. All the key stages on the critical path must, by definition, finish on time or the project schedule will slip.

For example, referring to the logic diagram in Figure 6.6, the available paths are:

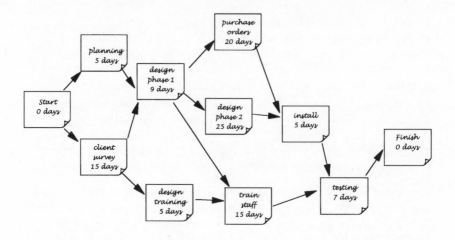

Figure 6.6 *The logic diagram with durations inserted (note durations are in consistent units).*

1. Start – planning – design phase 1 – purchase orders – install – testing – Finish: 37 d.
2. Start – planning – design phase 1 – design phase 2 – install – testing – Finish: 42 d.
3. Start – planning – design phase 1 – train staff – testing – Finish: 36 d.
4. Start – client survey – design phase 1 – purchase orders – install – testing – Finish: 56 d.
5. Start – client survey – design phase 1 – design phase 2 – install – testing – Finish: 61 d.
6. start – client survey – design phase 1 – train staff – testing – Finish: 46d.
7. Start – client survey – training design – train staff – testing – Finish: 42d.

So the critical path is number 5 in the list of available paths.

This is where reality hits you – is the project total time what your customer actually requires? If it is a long way out, do not worry yet as most project managers expect this to happen. Remember your estimates are based on people's perceptions. Your job is to attempt to compress the time to a schedule that is both real and achievable and satisfies your customer. To do this you need to make use of another valuable tool of project management – the *programme review and evaluation technique* (PERT for short). This tool allows you to analyse the logic diagram to confirm:

- the critical path – confirmation of your inspection;
- the start and finish times of all the key stages;
- the amount of 'spare time' available in the non-critical key stages.

All this data is very useful to you for optimising the project schedule, but more importantly for the control of the project work once this starts.

THE PROGRAMME EVALUATION AND REVIEW TECHNIQUE (PERT)

The PERT method of critical path planning and scheduling is the most commonly used technique for project management control. It is based on representing the activities in a project by boxes (or nodes) which contain essential information calculated about the project. The inter-dependencies between the activities are represented by arrows to show the flow of the project through its various paths in the logic diagram. The PERT diagram (sometimes referred to as a network) is identical to the logic diagram you derived earlier, each notelet for a key stage representing a node.

The conventional data stored in the node box is shown in Figure 6.7.

The four corners of the node box are used to store the four *characteristic times* for the key stage. These are calculated times using the durations derived in estimating – remember to keep all durations in the same units.

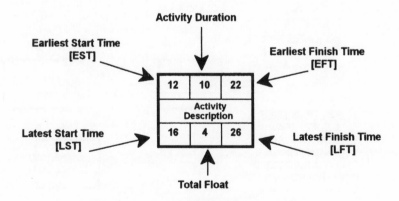

Figure 6.7 *The PERT node box.*

The lower middle box contains the *total float* for the key stage. This is the spare time in the key stage that allows you to take decisions about the actual start time or extending the duration within limits.

In Figure 6.7 the earliest start time is day 12 and the latest start time is day 16. This gives an option to start the activity any time between day 12 and day 16. The four-day difference is the spare time associated with the activity.

Starting anywhere in this time zone will not affect the total project time provided the activity is fully completed by the latest finish time of day 26. Say you were to start the activity on day 12 as the earliest planned date. If the time taken becomes extended from 10 days to 14 days, you use up all the spare time but maintain the total project time. If, however, the duration became extended to 16 days – two days more than the available spare time, you will extend the total project time by two days.

Obviously this process applies to every key stage and lower level activity in the WBS. If every key stage takes longer than the available spare time, the project will be very late. If the spare time is calculated as zero then that key stage is critical and one of those on the critical path. The PERT technique is founded on calculating

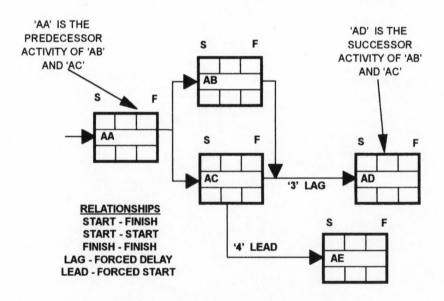

Figure 6.8 *Relationships in the PERT diagram.*

this information to permit you to take such decisions and control the project (see Figure 6.8).

The default or normal relationship used is 'finish' to 'start'. Under certain circumstances it is valid to impose constraints with the 'start' to 'start' or 'finish' to 'finish' relationships between activities.

You can impose a forced delay using a *lag* between the 'start' or 'finish' of a predecessor activity and the 'start' or 'finish' of one or more successor activities.

The forced start or *lead* is used to start a successor activity before the predecessor activity is completed.

Lags and leads should be used with care – it is easy to become confused and introduce errors. Split an activity instead of using leads to keep the diagram relatively easy to read and understand.

ANALYSING THE LOGIC DIAGRAM

The analysis of the diagram is a simple logical process extending the initial calculation you made earlier to locate the critical path.

Two steps are involved:

1. adding durations from start to finish – the forward pass;
2. subtracting the durations from finish to start – the backward pass.

Figures 6.9 through to 6.11 illustrate the technique.

As you can see the calculations only involve some simple arithmetic and you can easily carry out the analysis on the actual notelets you used to derive the logic diagram. In this way you and your team can quickly calculate the total project time and find those areas of the project where float time exists.

USING THE PERT ANALYSIS DATA

At this point in the planning process you may be looking at a plan that is giving you a total project time considerably longer than you really want. Do not despair – yet! Do not allow yourself to be tempted to go back and amend your time estimates. The next step is to convert the PERT data into a graphic format that is easier to work with and understand. This is the *Gantt chart* – a very useful tool for project work originally devised by Henry Gantt early in this century. At the time it was devised, Henry Gantt could not

STEP 1.
Decide the time each activity or Key Stage will take and enter these DURATIONS
on to the logic notes or BOXES.

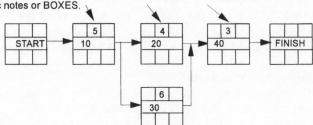

STEP 2
Number each box from START through to FINISH, working from left to right - numbers
or alphamerics.

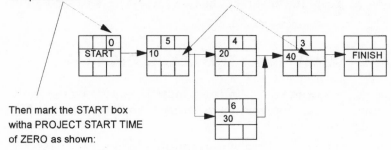

Then mark the START box
witha PROJECT START TIME
of ZERO as shown:

STEP 3
Transfer this TIME figure to the next box in the logic diagram:

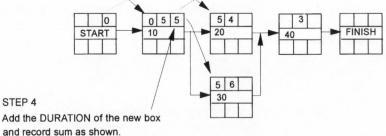

STEP 4
Add the DURATION of the new box
and record sum as shown.
Then transfer this time figure to the next box(es) in the diagram.

STEP 5
Repeat STEP 4 working through the LOGIC DIAGRAM from left to right.
When 'paths' meet, ensure you record the HIGHEST NUMBER into the next box.

Figure 6.9 *Analysing the project logic.*

The completed FORWARD PASS analysis now looks like this:

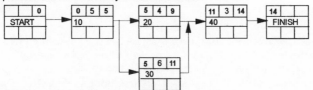

So we can conclude that the earliest time this small project can finish is 14 units of time.   The whole process is now reversed.

STEP 6
Transfer the finish time to the bottom corner of the box as shown.

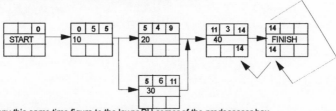

Then copy this same time figure to the lower RH corner of the predecessor box.

STEP 7
Subtract the activity DURATION from this time figure and enter the result in the lower LH corner of the same box.

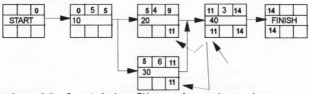

Then copy the result time figure to the lower RH corner of any predecessor boxes as shown above.
STEP 8
Continue step 7, copying the LOWEST TIME FIGURE to the next predecessor box where paths merge in the reverse pass.

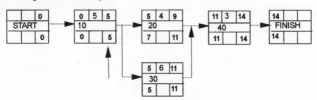

Figure 6.9 *Analysing the project logic (continued).*

The analysis of this logic diagram is now complete and the CRITICAL ELEMENTS can be clearly identified.

STEP 9

Look at each box in turn and identify those where the DIFFERENCE between the time figures in the UPPER and LOWER LH corners is EQUAL to the difference between the time figures in the UPPER and LOWER RH corners.

THESE BOXES IN YOUR DIAGRAM ARE THE CRITICAL ELEMENTS
AND FORM THE CRITICAL PATH OF THE LOGIC DIAGRAM.

A CRITICAL ACTIVITY

STEP 10

Finally enter the above calculated DIFFERENCE in the lower MIDDLE part of the box. This is the spare time or FLOAT TIME.

Then calculate the FLOAT times for all the boxes in the diagram:

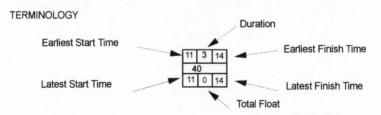

The LOGIC DIAGRAM analysis is now complete. Record the data in tabular format.

TERMINOLOGY

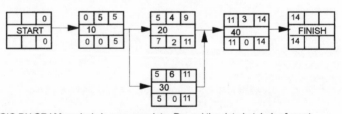

Figure 6.9 *Analysing the project logic (continued).*

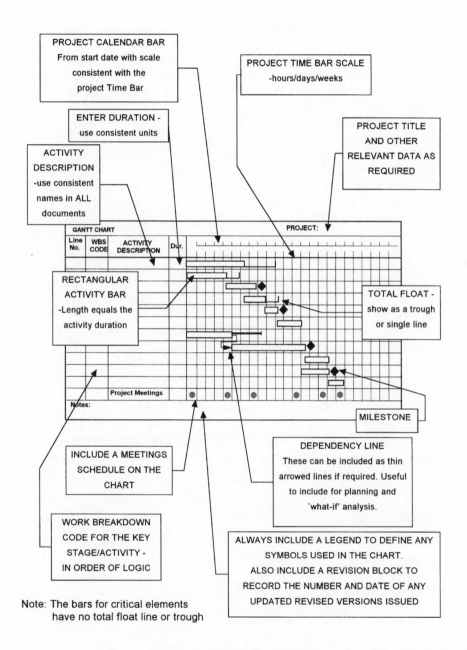

Figure 6.10 *The Gantt chart.*

have truly envisaged just how valuable his invention would become for project managers.

The Gantt chart and its various parts are shown in Figure 6.10.

The chart allows you to show a listing of all the key stages of the project, their durations and, if required, who is responsible. The chart is divided into two sections, a tabulated listing and a graphic display where each key stage is represented by a rectangle. All the rectangles are located on a timescaled grid to show their position in the schedule. It is useful to have both a project timescale bar and a calendar timescale bar across the top of the chart. This allows you to include the non-working days such as weekends and holidays. The key stages are listed on the left-hand side, by convention, in order of their occurrence in the logic diagram (working from left to right). List activities in such an order that the rectangles will appear on the chart to give a perception of flow. This is from the top left-hand corner to the bottom right-hand corner where project completion occurs.

You will note that the float time is also shown on the chart as a trough extension to those rectangles or bars (the common term) on the right-hand end, ie at the finish end of the bar. When you initially draw any Gantt chart the float is *always* drawn at this end. The limit of float is the limit of the time available if the schedule is not to be threatened and possibly extend the whole project. Of course critical activities have zero float and you can choose to highlight these with the use of colour.

The dependency links you have established in the logic diagram are not usually drawn on the Gantt chart, because they might cause some confusion in reading the document. However you can include them and this is readily done by using carefully drawn arrows on the chart, between the start and finish of the dependent activities (ignoring the float zone).

Eventually you will use the Gantt Chart to include some other useful information by adding some symbols to the diagram, but do not use any more than essential. This usually includes:

- *milestones* – special checkpoints usually indicated by a triangle or a diamond symbol;
- *project meetings* – indicated by a filled circle or dot;
- *project reviews* (ie financial/audit) – indicated by a filled square.

Remember to give a legend describing what the symbols mean!

The initial Gantt chart you produce at this stage is then opti-mised to reflect what you can achieve with available resources balanced with customer desires. This frequently involves com-pressing the schedule to reduce the time for the project. If there are no resources to do the work in the time scheduled the Gantt chart is a useless document expressing hopes and wishes! Analyse the resource requirements for the tasks in the plan and then optimise the schedule.

These steps may involve considerable reiteration to arrive at an acceptable solution – a process where project management soft-ware is very powerful. Small changes in the schedule are rapidly reflected in the chart and the logic simultaneously recalculated automatically. This allows you to carry out 'what if' analysis, viewing the impact of changing anything in your plan in a host of different ways. You can explore all available options you can think of to derive a finally acceptable schedule. This process is necessary to convince your customer and the project sponsor just what is realistically possible provided clear commitments of resources are made. Obviously this process is much more time-consuming manually!

ANALYSE YOUR RESOURCE REQUIREMENTS

You must now ask your key stage owners to validate the task list in their respective key stages using the techniques used earlier for the key stages. Much of the data will have been generated earlier but this now needs some closer analysis, particularly for the initial key stages.

Identify the resources most likely to be assigned the work and then working with them as an extended team:

- review the initial task list;
- add to the tasks where necessary;
- analyse for the 'often forgotten tasks':
  - documentation;
  - approval times;
  - testing planning and development;
  - project reviews and gathering the data;
  - project meetings;
  - replanning and planning reviews;
  - customer meetings;
  - user group meetings;
  - negotiations with suppliers;
  - expediting and purchasing administration;
  - training;

- inter-site travel and communication;
- updating project file records.

Suggest each key stage owner derives a complete list of tasks, then produces a responsibility chart for each key stage. Then they can estimate the durations of all the tasks in the key stage using the same techniques as before. Then identify the actual people who will carry out the work and confirm their commitment and availability. When you identify resources remember to review:

- previous experience;
- individual capabilities;
- technical knowledge;
- accuracy of their work;
- speed of working;
- capacity to do the work.

Use the same techniques as before to derive the logic diagram for all the tasks inside each key stage. Then determine its critical path and the total float available in the tasks. Some of these tasks may be assigned milestone status later. This enables you to produce a Gantt chart for each key stage. As the project continues you develop a complete family of such charts that are all expanded views of the primary or overall key stage Gantt chart. In this way a detailed plan of the work for a particular part of the project is clearly defined by the people doing the work and it minimises misunderstandings about responsibility. At the same time these people can confirm;

- the work can realistically be completed on time;
- resource capacity and availability;
- the line manager(s)' commitment to providing resources.

You now have the data to update the WBS. However, another advantage of this method is that the detailed work of a key stage does not need to be derived until a week or two before the work starts. This allows the planning to incorporate any unexpected outputs from earlier key stages. In this way you continuously work to hold your plan dates, seek the required resources and optimise your schedule to meet the total project time desired.

OPTIMISING YOUR SCHEDULE

The schedule is always based on the calendar, taking into account the non-working days during the project. Before attempting to optimise review the project brief to check that nothing is forgotten and the plan is aligned to stated objectives. The process of optimising a schedule is a team activity to create acceptance and commitment.

It involves taking decisions by consensus to maintain a balance between:

- the schedule – time;
- the resources available – cost;
- performance – scope and quality.

The options available are fairly limited when optimising trade-offs between these three to arrive at a solution. There is no perfect plan, only the best solution based on available information at the time. The options are:

- re-evaluate the dependencies in the logic for the key stages;
- review relationships – initially you used finish to start, now examine if other types give an improvement (see Figure 6.8);
- introduce lags and leads – with caution though;
- split key stages to get more concurrency;
- review assigned durations – remove or reduce contingencies added;
- review original estimates – realistically;
- seek more or different resources;
- seek to get current resource capacities increased – more time available;
- examine to ensure reinvention is minimised;
- reduce scope or quality or specifications – a last resort option.

Although it is sometimes tempting to use activity float times in optimising it is better to keep this option up your sleeve. Float time is not to be seen as an opportunity to stretch an activity to fill the available time. If you allow this to happen you create another critical activity by convention, so it is easy to turn everything critical by using up all float.

It is preferable to tell your team that float time is only used as a last resort with your consent (during the execution phase) to enable recovery planning when things go wrong.

Whatever solution you finally derive, do not forget to update the key stage Gantt chart and check the project risk log to identify if any risks have changed ranking.

With a final Gantt chart produced you must decide that there is no further improvement needed or it is the best result you can achieve. Before you go through the final steps of tidying up your project plan it is advisable to present this schedule informally to your customer and project sponsor to check if it is acceptable. If it is not, then you must seek alternative solutions through further optimisation. If the schedule is nominally agreed you can proceed to the final steps of planning before launching the actual work.

REVIEW YOUR PROJECT RISK LOG

Refer to your project risk log and review all the risks identified during the project definition phase. Ask:

- Have any changed status?
- Any new high risks? Identify actions on a risk management form.
- Any new risks identified from planning?

In reviewing risks it is tempting to avoid having any high risks listed – after all it saves paperwork – but is this reality? Remember, as project manager you are responsible for project performance. If you knowingly misrank a risk, who are you kidding? It could backfire on you later so carefully debate the quantifying and ranking of *all* risks with the team and agree a result. Identify the triggers for the risks identified.

Examine your plan to identify possible risk areas (refer back to Checklist 8):

- tasks on the critical path (and inside a key stage);
- tasks with a long duration (low capacity factors?);
- tasks succeeding a merge in the network;
- tasks with little float left (where is the float?);
- tasks dependent on third parties;
- lags and leads;
- start to start relationships;
- tasks using several people (particularly at different times);
- complex tasks;
- anything involving a steep learning curve;
- tasks using new or unproved technology.

Do not remove any risks from the log, if any are no longer likely to occur. Only remove the status ranking and leave these columns blank.

Prepare new action plans for any new high risks identified or those that have moved up in ranking. These are copied with the risk log appropriately dated into the project file and to the project sponsor. Assign responsibilities for day-to-day monitoring of risks to the key stage owners. Stress the importance of monitoring for the triggers that could signal a risk becoming an issue. Avoiding a risk is better than a damage limitation exercise later!

REVIEW YOUR PROJECT BUDGET

At this point, now that the base plan is complete and you are confident you have an acceptable schedule, review the project budget. Begin by updating the project WBS with all the lower level detail – or at least as much as you can at this stage. This is the easiest way to work out the cost of each based on:

- capital equipment costs;
- resource direct costs – based on cost rates;
- revenue costs for the project team – materials, expenses, etc;
- indirect costs – chargeable overheads etc.

With the costs of each key stage identified you can produce an operating budget as a cumulative amount aggregated against the schedule time. This is the real budget for project control purposes. If it varies significantly from the original approved budget you were given by the project sponsor then this variance must be investigated and the conflict resolved. If an increased cost is identified then the customer will need to be consulted for approval. Prepare for this discussion by deriving some alternative options as you did when optimising the schedule earlier.

Generally a small increase in cost has far less significant impact on the benefits than an increase in project time, particularly for new products. Keep a record of all costs for control measurement and variance analysis as your project proceeds.

SEEKING APPROVAL TO LAUNCH YOUR PROJECT

You have now completed the planning phase as far as necessary before launching the project work. At this point plan documentation comprises:

- a list of key stages;
- the project logic diagram;
- a project key stage responsibility chart;

CHECKLIST 13: A BASELINE PLAN CHECKLIST

Ask:

- Is the project brief still completely valid?
- Is the scope of work statement still valid?
- Has the project manager's authority been confirmed in writing?
- Are all stakeholders identified?
- Does the team understand who manages the stakeholders?
- Is the WBS developed as far as practicable?
- Does the WBS include all project administration tasks?
- Are customer and sign-off checkpoint meetings included?
- Is the critical path established and agreed?
- Are all key stages allocated for responsibility?
- Are key stage owners clear about their responsibilities?
- Is the project risk log complete and up to date?
- Are estimation records in the project file?
- Has a project calendar been established?
- Are resource loadings and capacities optimised and agreed?
- Does the Gantt chart reflect an agreed plan and schedule?
- Has the project operating budget been derived and approved?
- Does the team include all the skills needed?
- Has action been taken to acquire unavailable skills needed for the project?
- Are the team members working well together?
- Have any conflicts been resolved promptly and effectively?
- Is intra-team communication working well?
- Is the project sponsor performing in accordance with defined role?

Add additional questions to ask as appropriate.

- responsibility charts if appropriate for each key stage;
- a record of estimates for all the key stages;
- an optimised project Gantt chart for the key stages;
- Gantt charts for the early key stages or if possible all of them;
- an updated and reviewed project risk log;
- risk management forms for new high risks;
- a project operating budget.

Go through Checklist 13 to make sure you have not forgotten anything! The steps you have taken to arrive at this stage of the project are shown in the flow diagram in Figure 6.11.

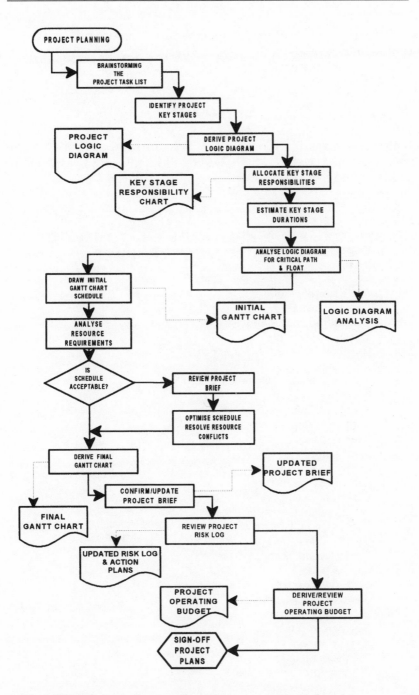

Figure 6.11 *Process flow diagram – project planning.*

Call the key stakeholders together for you to present these documents and explain the plan. Request them to approve the plan which you then 'freeze' as the baseline plan.

SUMMARY

Figure 6.11 gives the process flow diagram for the steps in planning the project. Checklist 14 summarises the key leadership actions to take during planning.

CHECKLIST 14: KEY LEADERSHIP ACTIONS DURING PROJECT PLANNING

■ *Project stakeholders:*
  - Gather relevant data.
  - Consult regularly with customer and end user.
  - Involve in planning.
  - Use their skills and experience.
■ *Project tasks:*
  - Confirm special skills required.
  - Prioritise the work.
  - Decide planning tools to use.
  - Confirm options.
  - Set standards.
■ *Project team:*
  - Involve in all aspects of planning.
  - Encourage creativity.
  - Structure as appropriate.
  - Focus on short-term priorities.
  - Encourage consensus.
  - Confirm roles.
  - Explain all decisions.
■ *Team members:*
  - Encourage participation.
  - Uncover past experience.
  - Listen to understand.
  - Respond to questions.
  - Agree personal targets.
  - Maintain enthusiasm and commitment.
  - Coach and develop skills.
  - Confirm responsibilities.

7

LAUNCHING YOUR PROJECT

Congratulations, your plan and schedule are approved. So now you are ready to start the project work. There are still a few activities you need to give some attention to before you hit the 'go' button. You produced a final Gantt chart for the key stages and analysed this for your resource needs when you optimised the schedule to meet the customer requirements. At this stage these resource requirements are not really a commitment. Certainly you may have received some promises from individuals and even their line managers but you cannot continue with the work based on just promises. You need to take such statements a stage further to be sure resources are available to you just when the plan tells you they are required. If the project sponsor has adequately stressed the context and priority of the project you can rely on this being clearly understood by all line managers providing resources and you will not be let down!

Are you really that confident? The key stage owners for the early key stages should have identified all the tasks to be carried out in each. This task list is the basis of ensuring you get the commitment you need.

ESTABLISHING KEY STAGE WORK PLANS

Consider what happens when you assign some work to someone. The first thing most people do is to work out how and when they are going to do the work, even if it is only a simple 'to do' list. So there is no reason why you cannot do this for them. Ask the key stage owners to verify their task lists, making sure they have not forgotten any tasks. If appropriate even get them to work out the logic diagram for the key stage using the same techniques you used earlier. Then record the task list on a *key stage work plan chart* as in Figure 7.1.

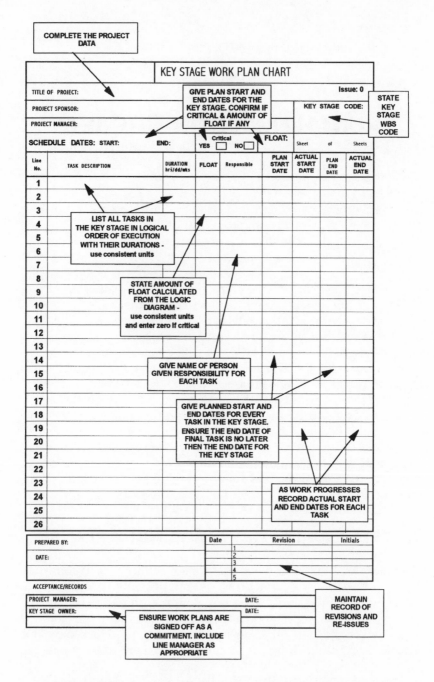

Figure 7.1 *An example of a key stage work plan chart.*

You will notice that this template records some important information for the key stage under consideration:

- the key stage code as recorded on the WBS;
- the key stage schedule start and end dates, whether it is a critical and calculated float;
- the duration of each task in the key stage using consistent units;
- the amount of float in each task if this has been calculated;
- the name of the person responsible for carrying out the task;
- the plan start and end dates for each task;
- a record of the actual start and end dates for each task.

Once the work plan is complete, confirm that all the tasks are:

- allocated to someone for responsibility;
- have plan start and end dates;
- are realistic and achievable within the total time planned for the key stage without using the float time.

Then submit the document for sign-off and approval by the key stage owner and yourself. This sign-off also allows you to verify that the task list does not:

- include tasks that you do not want done or consider unnecessary;
- omit some tasks that you consider essential to your project;
- have any obvious errors of estimating.

If the resources employed are not reporting to you full time, then get the work plan accepted and signed off by the line manager(s) involved as a commitment. Copy the work plans produced in this way to the people involved and their line managers. This reminds them of the contract they have concluded with you.

Of course the work plan may show that it is not possible to carry out all the tasks within the time allowed for the key stage. You must use your skill as a negotiator and influencer to seek a way to resolve the conflicts you can identify. Take the same approach to optimisation that you used when deriving your original Gantt chart. Your choices are limited but usually enough to come up with a satisfactory and acceptable solution:

- seek more resource capacity;
- obtain more resources;
- review and modify the logic inside the key stage;
- amend the scope or quality of the work.

The key stage work plan chart is also a convenient way to record the progress of tasks to completion.

This process may seem at first sight to be time-consuming and onerous. The people doing the work have to do some sort of plan. You are only asking them to use a consistent and disciplined approach to work planning. You do not need to produce all the key stage work plan charts at the outset, just those for the first few key stages. As the project continues, at any point, you can work proactively to prepare more work plans, taking into full account everything that has happened in the project. This is known as 'layering the plan' as the project proceeds. It is more effective and less time-consuming, minimising replanning of detail due to changes. If the logic diagrams for each key stage are worked out then turn these into individual Gantt charts for the key stages. This family of charts at the second level of planning should align with your overall key stage Gantt chart.

Having satisfied yourself that the early work plans are acceptable, you now need to decide where to locate the milestones of your project.

ESTABLISHING A MILESTONE SCHEDULE

Figure 7.2 shows the earlier diagram relating the schedule to risks and issues.

Replace 'schedule' with milestones, since these are all the significant events that are due to occur during the execution of the

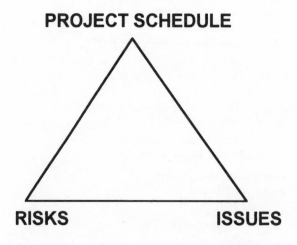

PROJECT SCHEDULE

RISKS   **ISSUES**

Figure 7.2 *The risks–issues–schedule triangle.*

project. Just like the lump of stone beside the highway the *milestone* is a flag or signal at some clearly defined point in the project. That signal indicates that something special should have happened or is about to happen. The milestone is therefore an instrument of control, effectively placing target points in the project schedule for certain events to be signed off as completed.

What are these events? Really they can be anything identified as a target that is significant in the project. However, this does not mean everything is a milestone.

Some of the common events given the status of project milestones are:

- completion of a key task, eg providing output to third parties;
- completion of one of the project deliverables;
- stage generation of benefits;
- completion of third party significant event, eg acceptance tests;
- completion of third party activity, eg delivery of equipment or data;
- a financial audit point;
- a project audit point;
- a quality audit;
- completion of a significant stage of work (possibly a critical element);
- a significant decision point, eg abort the project;
- completion of a project stage to release further funding – called a phase gate.

Each key stage owner must suggest where to locate the milestones in their key stage and agree these in a team meeting. The frequency of milestones in a network must be sufficient for effective control. Record the list of milestones on a schedule and on the Gantt chart. For effective control all milestones must be measurable with clearly established metrics – apply the SMART test.

See the example template for the milestone schedule in Figure 7.3.

Think of the milestones as the 'marker posts' to show the route to the finishing post – project completion. For a successful project you must reach each milestone on time or be prepared to explain why a slippage has occurred.

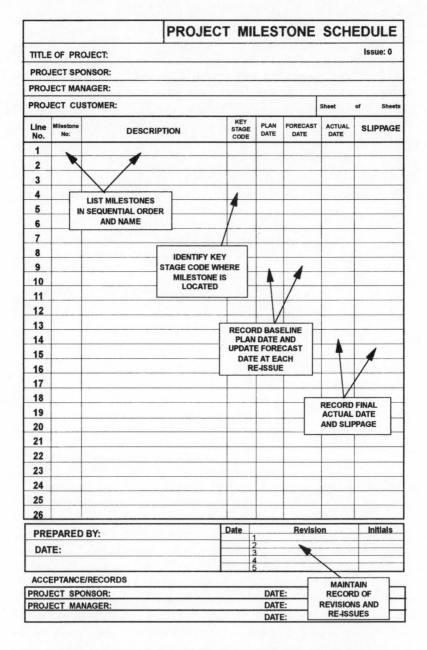

Figure 7.3 *An example of a project milestone schedule.*

CRITICAL SUCCESS FACTORS

You might be asked to identify the critical success factors (CSFs) for your project. These are a means of identifying progress towards a successful outcome and two types are relevant:

- process type;
- project type.

Process CSFs are those associated with the strategy you employ to achieve success. These include the tools, techniques, processes and procedures you use to define, plan, execute and complete the project on time, to the budget. Therefore they include:

- defining the project objectives, deliverables and benefits;
- ensuring the sponsor is appointed and sustains support and commitment to the project;
- the stakeholders are regularly consulted and kept informed of project status;
- an appropriate team is formed and the right skills are utilised;
- a carefully crafted and scheduled plan exists and is maintained up to date;
- control procedures for monitoring and tracking progress are understood by everyone;
- the WBS is maintained accurately as you continue to layer the plan;
- project sign-off and approval processes are maintained;
- project risks are regularly reviewed and monitored;
- project issues are resolved promptly at the appropriate level of management;
- reporting and communication procedures are established and working well.

Project factors are derived from the list of deliverables and benefits, particularly if the latter start to produce a yield before completion. Do not select all deliverables as CSFs, rather select just three or four. Identify those for which you can easily derive some metrics and agree how to measure progress. Although the budget is regarded as a measurable factor it is only one way of measuring progress and does not always signify success!

Whatever you select as a CSF, check it is acceptable to your key stakeholders – the customer and your project sponsor – as they can use this as a means of measuring performance.

ENSURING EFFECTIVE COMMUNICATION

Communication in project work is the glue that holds everything together! Poor communication is a major source of conflict and slippages so give this serious attention before you start the project work. Ask yourself:

- who needs to know;
- what do they need to know;
- how much do they need to know;
- how often must they be informed.

Establish distribution list(s) as appropriate but avoid generating large volumes of paper that few will ever read. The focal point for all communication is yourself. You must decide the ground rules you will impose on everyone involved to get prompt feedback of the prevailing situation with the work in progress. Effective monitoring and tracking of the project is dependent on good communication in the team, between you and the team and your key stakeholders. You need prompt feedback about:

- current progress of the active tasks;
- problems encountered with the work;
- problems anticipated with work waiting to be done;
- technical difficulties being encountered.

Reporting in a project environment requires you to have a continuous awareness of what is happening and what is due to happen next. Promptly identify any problems that interfere with progress. Potential changes to the plan that become apparent as a result of work in progress must be alerted to you. Lay out the ground rules for an early warning system – it can save a great deal of rework later and reduce the risk of replanning causing project delays. Agree the ground rules with your team so they all accept they are not being asked to do things they consider are unnecessary. Stress that you intend to operate an 'open door policy' – even if you do not have an office door! You are always willing to make time available to discuss difficulties and give help and guidance.

This effectively means you:

- are always ready to listen to their concerns and difficulties associated with meeting the schedule requirements;
- want regular verbal reports as well as documented reports of project progress;
- want to be informed promptly of any risks identified;

- need to be told if anyone anticipates a problem or risk occurring – however trivial it may appear to be.

Work with your team to create a climate for regular sharing of information in the interests of continuous improvement. Evaluate performance, not in order to blame when things do not go according to plan but to learn and improve performance.

Maintain everyone's focus on achieving the project objectives on time, to the budget and to the quality desired by your customer.

PROJECT STATUS REPORTS

Your key stakeholders expect to receive regular status reports. Decide the frequency of these with your project sponsor. In practice status reports are an administrative headache for many people. Some will avoid reports completely if possible, others will write a note of just a few lines. Some people are delighted to spend a whole afternoon compiling a thorough and detailed report blow by blow of everything they have done. It is an opportunity for literary abuse or verbosity so set the standard and quality you require. In today's electronic environment it is tempting to use e-mail and copy to almost the whole organisation! Tell the team what you expect of them irrespective of the methods employed. Long reports are often only scanned and not fully digested, with key issues being lost among the jargon and detail. Try to avoid jargon if reports are likely to go to people who have a different jargon dictionary to you and your team. Define your jargon clearly so there is no opportunity for misunderstandings to occur later.

Ask yourself just what you need to clearly define the current status of the project. Tell the team how you want these reports given and their frequency.

At any point in the project you want to know:

- what has been completed;
- what has not been completed and why;
- what is being done about the incomplete work;
- what problems remain unsolved;
- what needs to be done about these unsolved problems;
- what difficulties are anticipated in the work waiting to be done.

It is appropriate to use a single page standard template for reporting project progress, as shown in the example in Figure 7.4. You could use the key stage work plan charts although these are not focused enough for control purposes.

The project status report highlights progress using the milestones fixed earlier. The essential inputs to the report are:

- a concise summary of overall progress;
- a list of milestones due to be completed since the last report and their current status, ie on time, late, etc;
- a list of milestones due in the next reporting period, with their due dates;
- actions set in place to correct any slipped milestones;
- forecasts for the project completion based on current information;
- reasons for any revision to earlier forecasts to completion;
- changes to the project risk log and the project milestone schedule;
- any issues outstanding for resolution.

No one likes to hear bad news, but the sooner it is exposed the quicker you can react to limit the damages and take corrective action. You can use this template at any level in the project. Ask your key stage owners to use it to report progress on each key stage in this way. Similarly you can use the same template to report to the key stakeholders.

Agree the frequency of reporting with your project sponsor. If you are not confident of the veracity of any report you can soon investigate at a more detailed level. At least you are keeping the formal paper volume to a minimum.

Remember that issues arise from risks that actually happen, even if you failed to identify them as risks. Managing issues is discussed in detail in Chapter 8.

Throughout the project make sure everyone understands who is responsible for doing the separate parts of the project and give your support and guidance whenever it is needed. This includes securing the help of others when necessary in the interests of the project.

Good teamwork is directly related to effective and regular communication. The other element of communication you must consider is the meetings schedule.

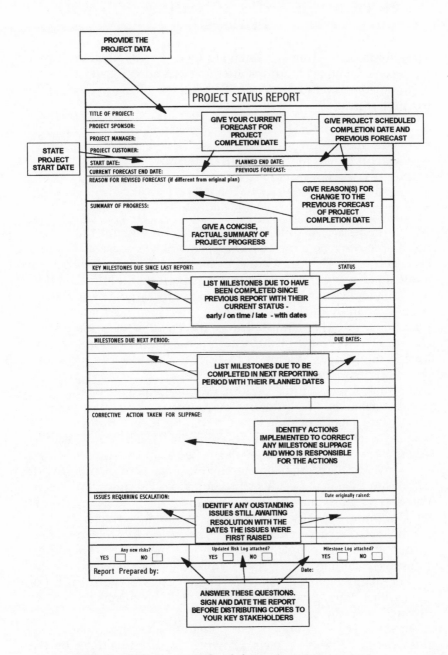

Figure 7.4 *An example of the project status report.*

DERIVE A MEETINGS SCHEDULE FOR YOUR PROJECT

The subject of meetings and making them effective is a topic that has received a huge amount of attention and numerous works exist to guide you. You must now decide what meetings are essential to the project process:

- one-to-one meetings with the project sponsor;
- one-to-one meetings with your team members;
- project progress meetings with the team;
- problem-solving meetings;
- meetings with particular stakeholders;
- project review meetings with the stakeholders.

All are necessary at different frequencies throughout the project but do not convene a meeting unless you have good reason and a clear purpose. The one-to-one meetings are very important to maintain close contact with your project sponsor and the members of your team. This is the only way you can really get to know these people as individuals and give and receive information at a personal level. This contributes to the creation of a motivating climate in your team, encouraging open communication and sustaining the focus on the project's success. It is also the forum for discussing problems and resolving issues of a more personal nature that impact on the performance of the project work.

Apart from giving guidance and support, you may need to coach team members sometimes, recognise their efforts and take actions to promote personal development. These are all actions you must take to build a successful project team. Set up a schedule in your diary for regular one-to-one meetings (say monthly) with each team member. Decide with your project sponsor how often you should meet and put these meetings in your diary. Allow 30–45 minutes for these informal one-to-one discussions.

Problem-solving meetings tend to be *ad hoc* as problems arise, involving specific people, which may not mean the whole team. Consider including other experts, invited to give help and advice. Do not mix problem-solving with progress or team meetings as the discussion easily gets out of control and the meeting becomes diverted from the purpose.

Agree a schedule of project progress meetings, preferably throughout the whole project, showing the schedule dates on the key stage Gantt chart. This does not mean you must hold such meetings. Then everyone knows they must be available to attend and not interpret any schedule date as an opportunity to take a day's holiday! If you have nothing to discuss, cancel or postpone any meeting. Decide the frequency to suit your needs and the size of the project. Weekly short meetings at the start or end of a week are good for small- to medium-sized projects if all the team are on the same site. If your team is multi-site the frequency is likely to be monthly so you must confirm you have opened other communication channels where appropriate – e-mail or video link meetings.

Project review meetings with your stakeholders are less frequent and usually involve you in preparing much more material to present formally to the group. Ideally limit these meetings to three or four in a 12-month period.

HANDLING PROJECT CHANGES

Yes, you are certain to face changes as the project proceeds! However carefully the plans are prepared there are certain to be some aspects of the work that produce some unexpected surprises. Uncontrolled change can sink the whole project. Minor changes appear during monitoring and are controlled by prompt reaction and taking corrective measures. Significant change is much more serious and must have a closer scrutiny before implementation is permitted. These changes can come from anywhere. A customer or end user can request a change because of changes to their needs or their working environment. A serious technical problem may signal a major change and cause replanning of the project and modify the objectives.

Any change that is expected to create a replanning activity and affect the total project time as currently scheduled must be handled in a formal manner. The primary elements of change management to consider include:

- source of the change request;
- the benefits from making the change;
- consequences of doing nothing at this stage;
- cost impact of making the change;
- effect on project constraints;
- effect on resource needs;
- increase or decrease in project risks;
- effect on the objectives and scope of the project.

Major change can have a demotivating effect on the team unless it is something they have sought in the interests of the project. These changes are not implemented until after careful consideration of the consequences to the project and even other active projects. A major change on one project could have a serious impact on the resource availability for another project. All major changes must be approved by the customer and the project sponsor before action is taken to replan. In most situations some work is necessary to examine alternative solutions and their impact on the schedule before an agreement is reached with the customer.

A standard template is preferred for change requests. An example is given in Figure 7.5.

HOLD A LAUNCH MEETING

Now you have prepared everything you need to launch the project. The final steps after completing the baseline plan include:

- preparing work plan charts for the early key stages;
- deriving a milestone schedule for the project;
- deciding a progress reporting process with the templates everyone must use;
- agreeing a meetings schedule.

This launch meeting is a milestone in your project. It is the point from which all project work starts. Your purpose is to get together all the important people who are involved with your project and explain the plans in some detail. Decide whom you want to attend:

- the project sponsor;
- the customer;
- other key stakeholders – line managers providing you with resources;
- the project team.

Prepare yourself and your team well for the meeting. This is an important opportunity for you to explain the plan and the areas of high risk to achieving success. You are looking for acceptance from all those present that the project is well planned. You must convince them that with their cooperation you can achieve the objectives. Consider preparing a document package containing:

- the project organisation chart;
- the project stakeholder list;
- the key stage Gantt chart;
- the key stage responsibility chart;
- the project brief;
- any other relevant information;

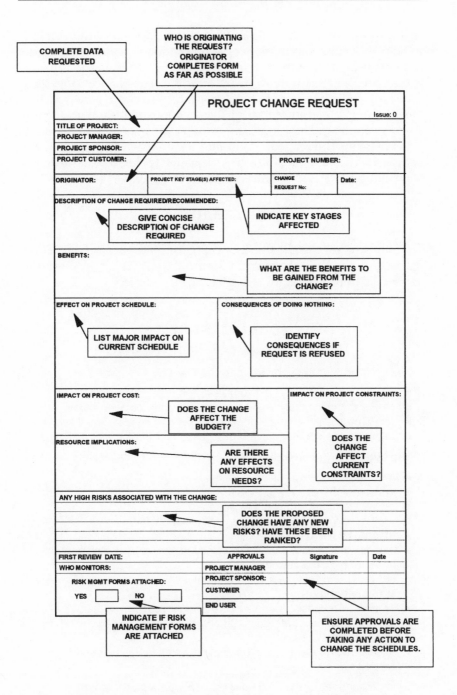

Figure 7.5 *An example of the project change request.*

You can issue this information pack to participants at the meeting to help gain their commitment. No one can later complain they do not understand the project plan or what you are trying to achieve. It is an ideal opportunity for team building. The chances of getting the team and stakeholders together in a project are rare and this meeting helps them understand their responsibilities in an organisational context. This is an important event so make it special, provide some lunch – if your budget allows! This encourages people to mix and talk together and get to know each other – contributing to good cooperation in the future.

SUMMARY

The steps you take in the launching of your project are summarised in the flow diagram in Figure 7.6. Checklist 16 gives the key leadership actions for this phase of the project.

CHECKLIST 15:
THE PROJECT LAUNCH MEETING

Ask your project sponsor to open the meeting to:

- explain the context of the project in the organisation strategy;
- stress the priority of the project against other active projects;
- focus on the importance of cooperation and support at all levels;
- reinforce the communication processes needed for success.

You take over the chair to:

- introduce the project team;
- introduce the information pack;
- briefly explain the project background;
- confirm the project objectives and deliverables;
- identify all the project benefits;
- explain the baseline plan, focusing on the critical elements, the areas of high risk and the schedule dates;
- set the ground rules for the communication processes, particularly status reporting;
- confirm everyone's understanding of their responsibilities;
- accept any relevant ideas and suggestions for improving the chances of success;
- respond to questions, and be committed to any questions that you cannot answer.

Celebrate the project launch – provide a buffet lunch!

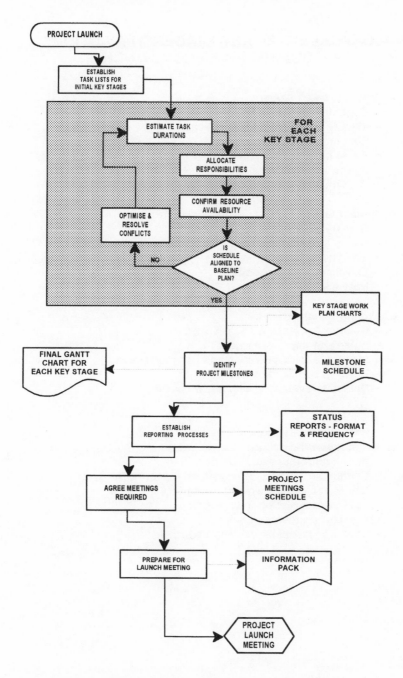

Figure 7.6 *Process flow diagram – project launch.*

CHECKLIST 16: KEY LEADERSHIP ACTIONS DURING PROJECT LAUNCH

■ *Project stakeholders:*
 – Confirm acceptance of schedule.
 – Identify functional roles in execution.
 – Agree reporting procedures.
 – Agree meetings schedule.
 – Clarify stakeholder responsibilities.
 – Confirm resource priorities and commitments.

■ *Project tasks:*
 – Confirm work plans are completed.
 – Clarify project objectives.
 – Explain the plan.
 – Explain control procedures.
 – Hold a launch meeting.

■ *Project team:*
 – Confirm key stage responsibilities.
 – Agree and approve all work plans.
 – Monitor team cooperation and communication.
 – React to conflict and resolve.
 – Celebrate the launch with a team activity.

■ *Team members:*
 – Encourage participation.
 – Recognise their efforts.
 – Act on grievances and concerns.
 – Confirm acceptance of short-term responsibilities.
 – Check non-project work commitments.
 – Guide and assist when appropriate.
 – Appraise performance.
 – Review personal targets and objectives.

8

EXECUTING THE PROJECT WORK

After all the enthusiasm demonstrated at the launch meeting you believe everyone is highly motivated and plunging into the project work. The reality is sometimes the opposite! After all the effort put into planning there is sometimes an 'adrenalin dip' when the team feels they should be doing something but nothing appears to happen! This is where you need to show your skills as a leader. Immediately after the launch meeting, call the team together for a very short team meeting. Give encouragement to reinforce the motivational level in the team. Check that there are no concerns, uncertainties or misunderstandings about the initial, scheduled work. Ask them to tell you if any problems occur. Remind them to watch out for new risks and any signals that suggest a risk is likely to happen and create an issue.

One of the most difficult areas of project work is new information coming in to the team members after the work starts. This is sometimes quite casual through informal meetings in the corridor, staff restaurant or even the car park. It may come from lower level sources in the customer's organisation. The input is also intentional on occasions and could have profound effects on the work, the schedule and team motivation. Changes to the plan are often started because of this type of information flow. You must guard against any input creating more work than necessary and remind team members to inform you immediately of such situations.

You are asking your team to keep you informed of progress, so when additional information appears you (and the team members) must question the source:

- Where does the information come from?
- Why was it not exposed before?
- Who has decided it is relevant now?

- Is the information accurate and realistic?
- Is there some hidden agenda associated with the timing?
- What impact does it have on the plan and schedule?
- Does this change the project objectives, deliverables or benefits?

Project work can be seriously constrained, or even sabotaged, by the subtle transfer of erroneous information to a team member. A complete absence of information when it is due to appear can have similar sinister origins. You are flexible in your approach to the project and always ready to consider changes to your plan when essential. If the information and data essential to the project work is confused by mixed messages from different people in the customer's organisation, this leads to conflict and confusion. Prepare your team for these events because they are certain to occur at some time in the project's life – if you have not experienced them already!

Your early warning system is the best way to get feedback about what has happened and what needs to happen. This provides you with the information to control the project.

THE PROJECT CONTROL SYSTEM

Control of a project environment involves three operating modes:

- *measuring* – determining progress through formal and informal reporting;
- *evaluating* – determining the cause of deviations from the plan and how to react;
- *correcting* – taking actions to correct.

These form the essential elements of your control system. The plan and schedule are the foundation that determines what has to be done to satisfy the objectives set out in the project brief. Your objective is to regulate the activities, resources and events to achieve the results defined by the plan. Control is associated with the present, so reporting is time-sensitive to enable prompt decisions when deviations occur. If all reporting mechanisms give feedback a considerable time after the event, as a matter of history, then you cannot control your project. The communication processes you designed during the project launch are designed to give timely visibility to significant events.

System design

No amount of time and effort expended on planning, scheduling and resource assessment will compensate for a lack of effective monitoring and a sound control system. The purpose of this system is to ensure that you and the team always have the information to make an accurate assessment of:

- *what has happened* and compare this with
- *what should have happened* according to the plan.

You compare these two inputs to establish if there is a variance. The best control system is the simplest – making the procedures and collection of data complex only leads to higher costs and an increasing possibility of error. The basic inputs to control are the plan and the actual results observed and measured by the team.

Figure 8.1 shows the essential elements of any control system. The comparison activity should show whether the project is on track and everything is going according to plan. If this is true you can update the project records and charts and report progress to your customer and project sponsor. If progress is not to plan then it is important to identify the causes of any problems that are creating delays. Then develop solutions, preferably deriving several options before selecting the best or most appropriate. Prepare and implement an action plan to correct the difficulties and restore the project to the planned schedule. It is essential to measure the impact of action plans to provide feedback in the system and a check that the solution has worked.

Your control system must be capable of providing information on:

- The resource required – availability and its effective use;
- Equipment and machinery required and used;
- Materials used, ordered and required;
- The costs incurred to date and forward commitments;
- The time used and float time remaining in active tasks;
- The results achieved – tasks completed;
- A valuation of the results – as expected?

Controlling the project means managing the many problems that arise to maintain the project schedule. You do this on a day-to-day basis through:

- monitoring the work – observing and checking what is happening;
- identifying and resolving the problems that arise;

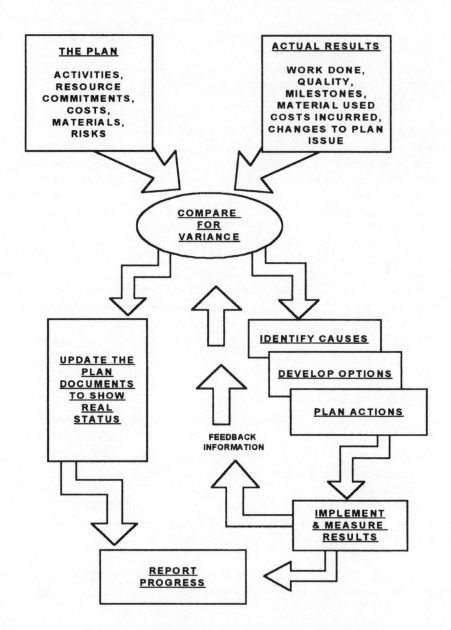

Figure 8.1 *The essential elements of a control system.*

- tracking the project – comparing with the plan and updating the records.

Although these are continuous activities the schedule is easier to track if you use some additional specific control points. The milestone schedule gives you the clearly defined markers for control throughout the project. Focus the team on these marker points, stressing the importance of maintaining the dates. Tell the team you must know if any milestone date is expected to slip. Remind them that the total float is not spare time for them to use by choice without reference to you.

One of the most time-consuming activities in project work is the administration. Good control of any process is dependent on accurate data, so make a special effort to keep the project file up to date. This involves a regular check and update of:

- the project organisation chart;
- the stakeholder list;
- the key stage responsibility charts;
- the project brief;
- the key stage Gantt chart;
- the key stage work plan charts;
- the project risk log.

Depending on the size of the project you can speed up the administration process using a project management software package – once you are familiar with its many features! Keeping the project file up to date is an obligation you must fulfil. You could be moved to another project at any time and someone else has to take over. Do ensure that the legacy you leave behind is a good one, otherwise you will continually be subject to queries and requests that interfere with your new role.

MONITORING PROGRESS

Although you have made a particular effort to set up effective communication processes do not rely on them always working effectively to give all the progress information. Confidence in progress reports only comes from verifying them from time to time. This obliges you to monitor:

- the team;
- the stakeholders;
- performance.

CHECKLIST 17: DESIGNING THE CONTROL SYSTEM

Ask:

- How is the work actually controlled now?
- Do you have budgets for hours and costs?
- Do you have data comparing actual hours/costs with planned hours/cost?
- How is the quantity of completed work measured and compiled?
- Is completed work related specifically to hours used or based on forecasts?
- How long does reported information take to get to you after the close off?
- How long does reported information take to get to you after the close off?
- How much time/cost is spent between close off and receipt of reports?
- What action do you take after reading the report?
- Can you take action based upon information in the report?
- Is reported information reasonably accurate? If not, why not?
- Who receives copies of the report? Why them? Can they take action? Do they?
- Can you list who receives the reports for information only?
- Who can take action to reduce costs, but do not receive reports?
- Has someone been assigned responsibility for each piece of work in the plan?
- Does the system provide a way to reduce key variables such as hours, costs, etc?
- Does the system focus on profit, time, quality, completion or on more than one of these?
- Do the system reports and rewards motivate the desired behaviour?
- Does it allow time/cost/quality trade-off decisions to be made quickly?
- Does the system include an early warning system to identify risks and issues?

You cannot do this effectively from behind a desk – you need to walk about, observe and have conversations! This is your data gathering process, which if done effectively is far more useful then any written report. Still demand the written reports, they are a valuable discipline for everyone working on the project as well as providing a historical record. Monitoring is a checking activity – talking to the team members and finding out directly how things are going. This is encouraging to the team and shows you care about them and their work. Too much monitoring is sometimes interpreted as interference, so there is a fine balance between the two extremes. Monitoring is also an opportunity to check that promised resources are in fact working on project tasks and are not diverted to other activities. Your visibility to the team also creates a climate where you rapidly learn about concerns and difficulties.

Decide the frequency

Are you content to rely on team meetings as the focal point of reporting project progress? This depends on how often you can afford to get the team together and your style of conducting these meetings. You must decide how often you intend to:

- walk about to observe what is happening – daily/twice weekly/weekly?
- hold one-to-one meetings with the customer and the project sponsor;
- hold one-to-one meetings with the team members;
- measure progress of key stage tasks;
- receive local reports – verbal and written – from key stage owners.

Many projects benefit from having regular short team meetings at the same time and day each week. This does depend on the team member's location and less frequent meetings are the only way of ensuring attendance. Less frequent meetings of the team puts a greater emphasis on frequent monitoring to check that the team are communicating with each other effectively. Regular monitoring demonstrates your concern for success and reinforces messages about watching out for new risks or anticipating future problems.

Measuring progress is always a difficult area for most people to define. Ask anyone how the work is going and the common response is 'OK, everything is coming along fine.' The reality is they probably haven't started yet! If you establish well-defined metrics to measure the progress, you soon know the project status. Agree the metrics with the people doing the work, the frequency of recording and stress the importance of using them effectively. Try to determine what tangible outputs come from a task or group of tasks and ask how these are measured by the people doing the work. After all they must have an idea how they are going to confirm when the tasks are completed! This data is essential to value the work completed at any point and check that the results achieved are in accordance with the plan. If unusual or unexpected results appear you need to be informed promptly so that corrective action can be decided. Figure 8.2 gives you the essential steps in the normal monitoring process.

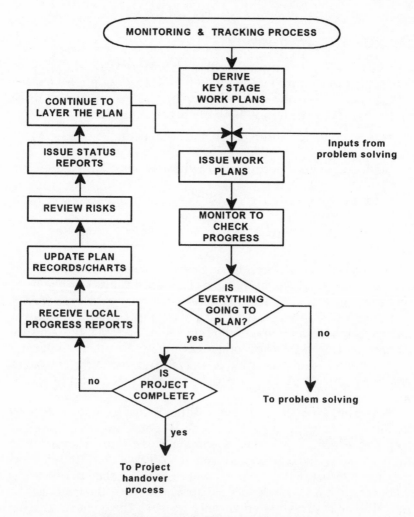

Figure 8.2 *The normal monitoring process.*

Reviewing the project risks

You have a project risk log updated at the close of the planning phase of your project. Throughout the execution phase you must keep a watch for risks that:

- are about to happen – and become an issue;
- are new – not identified earlier;
- have changed their ranking – high–medium–low;
- are no longer perceived as relevant.

It is useful to carry out a short review of risks at each team meeting. However, make sure the team understands that the steps involved in risk reviews are not confined to a meeting. They are a state of mind and must be part of the day-to-day work of each member of the team. You need to know about new risks anticipated or identified at the time they are recognised. The formal risk review is a team activity to use the experience and skills of the team members. If appropriate involve others with relevant expertise to help the team.

CHECKLIST 18: REVIEWING PROJECT RISKS

Steps in risk review:

- Check if any risks are no longer valid – remove the ranking completely but leave the risk on the list for future reference.
- Use the risk ranking matrix to verify the rankings of all risks on the list – raise or lower the rankings by consensus agreement in the team.
- Prepare risk management forms for any risks revised to 'high' ranking.
- List any new risks identified from current work and new work plan charts.
- Use the risk ranking matrix to rank new risks.
- Prepare action plans for any risks ranked as 'unacceptable'.
- Implement the action plans promptly.
- Prepare risk management forms for new 'high' risks.
- Ensure everyone knows the triggers that signal high risks becoming issues.
- Confirm or allocate responsibility for managing the risks on the list.
- Update the project risk log and issue to key stakeholders and the team.

The review process follows a number of discrete steps using the last issue of the project risk log.

Continue to remind the team at intervals of the risks that are particularly relevant at each stage of the work and maintain regular contact with your project sponsor for support. You know that risks become issues when they actually happen and a process for the prompt handling of these issues is essential.

MANAGING ISSUES

The purpose of the issue management process is to make sure all risks that happen are resolved promptly to avoid and/or limit damage to your project.

An issue is defined as:

> ... any event or series of related events (that may have been previously identified as a risk) that have become an active problem causing a threat to the integrity of a project and/or related projects.

Managing issues is similar to managing the original risks, requiring you to:

- keep records of all issues that occur;
- ensure action planning is promptly used to resolve the issues.

It is valuable to record issues to focus the team and others on learning from the corrective actions taken. It helps to prevent issues recurring on projects in the future. Although your primary concern when dealing with an issue is to get an action plan in place and implemented, a disciplined approach to planning action is important. It is too easy to overreact, 'shoot from the hip' and action the first idea you think of as a solution. This is not always the best solution and ignores the team's expertise in deriving an answer to the problem.

It is a good idea to record issues as they happen on an issue status log, a complete list of all issues raised on the project giving:

- issue name and source;
- who owns it;
- which parts of the project are affected;
- who is responsible for action plans to resolve it;
- a record of current ranking;
- when action is complete.

Design a template similar to the project risk log if appropriate. Issues are identified through regular monitoring. Since you have limited authority it is unlikely you can resolve all the issues without support from your project sponsor or even higher management. To enable a simple process, the issues are ranked using a traffic light system.

Ranking issues

Issues raised are ranked according to their impact and anticipated consequences by assigning a red, yellow or green flag:

Red flag	Major issue having serious consequences for the project. Prompt action needed to implement a decision to resolve. Overdue resolution of yellow flags.
Yellow flag	Significant impact on the project and/or other projects. Unless resolved promptly will cause delays to milestones. Becomes red if action delayed more than two days.
Green flag	Consequences limited to confined area of the project and unlikely to impact other projects. Becomes yellow if not resolved in time to avoid project slippage.

Any outstanding issues are identified when reporting progress of the project. You must also ensure that the ranking of any issue has not changed. It is important to keep your key stakeholders informed on progress with resolving issues, invoking their active support when necessary in the interests of the project.

Like the risks on the project risk log, no issues are normally removed from the log, even after resolution – the list is a valuable source of learning for future projects.

Escalation of issues

As you do not always have authority to decide all the actions to resolve issues arising during project work it is essential to establish defined responsibilities for the escalation of issues:

- Any issues given a 'green flag' are the responsibility of the project manager to resolve.
- Any issues given a 'yellow flag' are the responsibility of the project sponsor to resolve.
- Any issues given a 'red flag' are escalated to the senior management to decide the appropriate actions to implement and by whom.

In most situations you attempt to resolve the issue or consult your project sponsor without involving senior management. If the issue is ranked 'red' then it is referred to senior management for a decision. You are close to the problem so if this happens, expect to be asked for suggested actions to resolve the issue. A convenient way to focus on the essential elements of issue resolution is to use a standard checklist or standard template, particularly for the serious issues ranked 'red'.

The *issue management form* is a typical template (see Figure 8.3) to check all aspects of an issue are carefully analysed before seeking a decision. This allows you to identify more than one way of resolving the issue, offers senior management a choice of solutions and focuses on:

- areas of the project affected and consequences forecast;
- consequences if not resolved;
- proposed actions to resolve the issue with cost and resource implications;
- current ranking of the issue.

Always confirm that responsibility is clearly allocated for actions planned to avoid confusion when action is implemented. Finally check that each possible solution is analysed for potential risks. Too often a 'quick fix' solution may seem perfect in the short term, but introduce additional risks to the project later.

TRACKING YOUR PROJECT

It is essential to keep the project moving along the right track. To achieve this requires:

- that project control and monitoring tools are appropriate to the type of project;
- that the project team performs to the highest standards possible and responds to the changing needs of the project as data is generated by the control system;

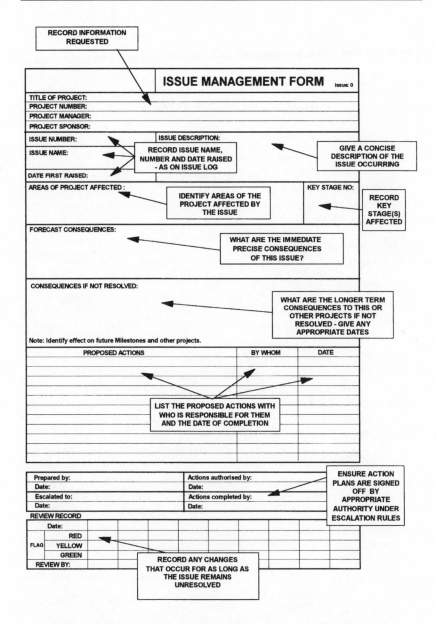

Figure 8.3 *An example of a project issue management form.*

- that the stakeholders remain committed to the project and promptly respond to changes perceived to be necessary for the successful completion of the project.

Tracking is the process by which the project progress is measured through monitoring to ensure that:

- the work is carried out in the right order as stated in the plan;
- planned performance is maintained – to agreed quality standards;
- the team are well motivated and committed to completing their individual work plans on time and within budget.
- changes to the plan caused by problems or the customer are promptly acted upon;
- the reported progress data is used to update the plan charts and records in the project file.

This normally involves working with the WBS and the key stage Gantt chart to show the real status of the project – the tasks that are on time and those that have slipped. To do this you must have a starting point or baseline to show the variances.

The baseline for all tracking is the project plan devised before implementation, where all key stages are fixed and responsibilities are clearly defined and accepted by the team members. The final key stage Gantt chart is the project baseline which *remains unchanged* throughout the project. As the work is done you mark progress on the chart by filling in the bars to show the amount of work completed – see Figure 8.4.

If a key stage is late starting, takes longer to complete or the finish suffers a delay, this is shown clearly on the chart. The original position of the bar on the chart is unchanged, as changing this modifies the baseline. Although this covers up the change that has taken place you lose the opportunity later to ask why it happened and what everyone has learned from the difficulties leading to the change.

Modifications to the plan are recorded as they occur to enable the experience to be logged for future projects. This may involve moving one or more tasks away from the original baseline position. This appears odd on the chart and tempts you to move the baseline with the comment: 'Well we never actually expected it to happen like that!' When you move anything on the Gantt Chart you are effectively modifying the project strategy for a reason.

The reason for a change must have a purpose and leaving the baseline unchanged forces you to fully document the changes to the plan and schedule. Later you evaluate the key learning points from the project and all these changes that occur. Of course if any of these modifications applies to critical key stages or tasks then

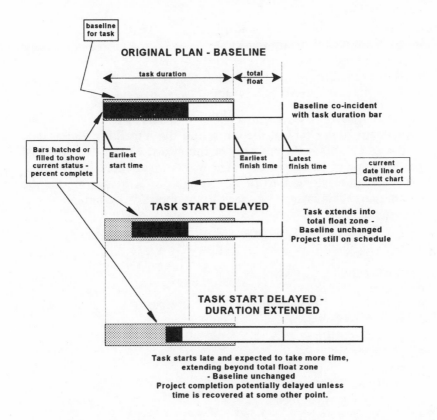

Figure 8.4 *Showing current status on the Gantt chart.*

the project completion is likely to be delayed. You then face the difficult task of recovery planning to try to get back to the original project schedule or persuade the customer to accept the extended completion date.

Deciding what completion means

Ask anyone engaged in project work how they are getting on and you can expect a reply like: 'Fine, I'm about halfway through.' What does this really mean? Is it really true that the work is 50 per cent complete? It is probably a guess that, depending on the individual, may be accurate or well wide of the real situation and just gives information you expect to hear!

The bar on a Gantt chart is a linear graphical representation of effort. In real life effort is never linear and depends on:

- the accuracy of the detailed planning of tasks to do;
- the complexity of the work;
- the amount of interruptions to the work;
- the availability of data and equipment;
- how the individual feels on the day.

The well proven 80/20 rule applies – 80 per cent of the results come from 20 per cent of the effort and the remaining 20 per cent of the results takes 80 per cent of the effort! Completing the last part of a piece of work can often take considerably longer than expected and extend into or beyond the total float zone on the Gantt chart. This brings you back to the metrics you agreed to use to measure progress.

Unfortunately there are nearly always forgotten tasks that take a significant amount of time to complete:

- documentation;
- approval times;
- planning and developing test procedures;
- project reviews;
- project meetings;
- planning reviews;
- replanning meetings;
- customer meetings;
- user group meetings;
- negotiations with suppliers;
- expediting;
- searching for information;
- purchasing administration;
- training;
- travel and communication;
- updating project records.

Most of these and others will happen and occupy time assigned to project work. They will interfere with the effort given to planned tasks and are often ignored when assessing the percentage completion. You presume that all tasks will be completed on time using the durations entered into the schedule. Don't ask for percentage completion assessments when seeking progress data. These assessments are rarely accurate because of their historical basis. You need to know whether the task will finish on time so ask for a forecast when it will be completed. This focuses the individual responsible for the work to review other commitments due in the same period and give a more realistic assessment of the time to complete.

If the forecast completion date is then clearly unacceptable when compared to the schedule, you have the opportunity to take some prompt corrective action. You should persuade all your key stage owners to get into the habit of forecasting performance for their key stages. This proactive approach highlights potential problems before they have a serious impact on the project, allowing you to focus on corrective action.

In addition forecasting has two other benefits:

- it improves everyone's ability to estimate time to do the work – forecasting is a 'real time' activity, not looking into a crystal ball for the distant future;
- it creates real targets for the individual doing the work – any delay beyond an agreed target cannot be tolerated.

The project status report (see Chapter 7) specifically requests these forecasts be given when reporting, along with reasons for any changes to previous forecast completion dates. Encourage the team to use these reporting templates and stress the importance of developing expertise in accurate forecasting. The analysis for variances at all stages must be a primary concern for the whole team, making sure effective corrective action is taken when problems and hold-ups occur.

Good monitoring and tracking builds team confidence, anticipates problems and prepares future success.

CHECKLIST 19: MONITORING AND TRACKING

The main criteria for effective tracking are:

- work content – is it to estimates, both time and cost?
- measurement – is everyone clear how to measure progress?
- timescales – are work plans being completed on schedule?
- quality – are standards being met in accordance with specifications?
- teamwork – are responsibilities being adhered to?
- changes – are problem-solving tools being used effectively?
- stakeholders – are they being kept informed, consulted and involved?

Pay particular attention to:

- having regular contact with team members;
- having regular contact with the customer and project sponsor;
- encouraging rapid feedback of progress and problems;
- dealing with difficulties promptly;
- responding to requests for guidance and help;
- maintaining good communication with team and stakeholders;
- focusing everyone on watching out for risks;
- keeping the project records and file updated;
- issues arising:
  - resourcing problems;
  - technical problems;
  - scheduling problems due to poor estimating;
  - responsibility conflicts;
- checking agreed action plans are effectively implemented;
- keeping everyone informed of project status.

TAKING CORRECTIVE ACTION

The monitoring and tracking process identifies the problems that are interfering with the schedule and indicate the need for some action. The analysis for variance should help to expose the causes of the problem, then use problem-solving tools to derive an acceptable solution.

Taking corrective action has limited possibilities:

1. Rearranging the workload(s) if a milestone is going to be missed – find others to take some of the tasks to relieve the loading or even reallocate the tasks.
2. Put more effort into the job – not an easy option to demand in practice.
3. Put additional resources into the job – resource constraints may negate this option.
4. Moving the milestone date – subject to the stakeholders' approval and time recovery later in the project; difficult with activities on the critical path.
5. Lower the scope and/or quality of the results demanded by the plan – only possible with agreement of the customer.

Corrective action is normally approached using these options in this order. Record any assumptions you make when deciding action plans – they could have a significance later! Before implementing any corrective actions carry out some simple checks that you have selected the best option based on the available information.

CHECKLIST 20:
TAKING CORRECTIVE ACTION

- Use cause and effect analysis to identify the problem cause.
- Use brainstorming techniques to find the possible solutions.
- Use the expertise of the team and others.
- Identify the most flexible area out of scope, cost or schedule.
- Select the two or three most acceptable solutions.
- Record all assumptions.
- Derive list of actions to implement the selected options.

Before deciding which option to use check if:

- the critical path has changed;
- any individual workloads are adversely affected;
- any milestones are subject to slippage;
- any new 'high' risks are exposed;
- any new issues are exposed;
- any cost overruns are introduced – do these need approval?;
- any localised schedule slippages are controllable – recoverable later?

When selecting the option and setting the action plan identify:

- the priority order of the tasks involved;
- who is responsible for carrying out the actions;
- who is monitoring the action plan implementation;
- what is the target completion date;
- who must be kept informed of progress.

PROBLEM-SOLVING

Project work inevitably is faced with an astonishing range of problems. Some would regard problems as just a challenge to overcome! In the project a problem exists if you:

- are faced with an unacceptable gap between what you currently have and what you desire as an outcome;

- are unable to see an immediate way to close or remove the gap.

For example, problems in your project can be about:

- the schedule – work takes longer than planned;
- the effort planned – tasks are not carefully detailed to derive accurate estimates;
- resources not available when promised;
- technical difficulties – technology doesn't work or is inadequate;
- inadequate training of team members – skills are not available;
- unforeseen absence of resources, equipment or materials;
- inadequate control – monitoring is not working effectively;
- failures in communication leading to misunderstandings and conflicts.

Much of your time goes into controlling the project schedule and taking prompt action when something unpredictable happens. If everyone focuses on risk management, you can hopefully minimise the number of unpredictable events. When they do occur you are faced with a problem that is treated as an issue to be resolved. Problem-solving is dependent on a sequence of logical steps, as shown is Figure 8.5.

Identifying the problem

It is important to frame the right problem. With the team agree a statement that clearly describes the perceived problem. This may change later after data gathering is complete. Getting a consensus agreement of this statement is important as it must embrace everyone's perception of the problem. Avoid pre-judging the causes and reasons for the problem occurring now.

Gathering data

Collect information about the perceived problem. Collecting data helps to analyse the problem and confirm you are looking at the real problem and not a symptom of a deeper, hidden difficulty. You have limited time to resolve the problem and sometimes have to take decisions with information of doubtful accuracy. Usually a better solution is possible if some time is devoted to collecting data using sampling techniques to count or measure the data needed.

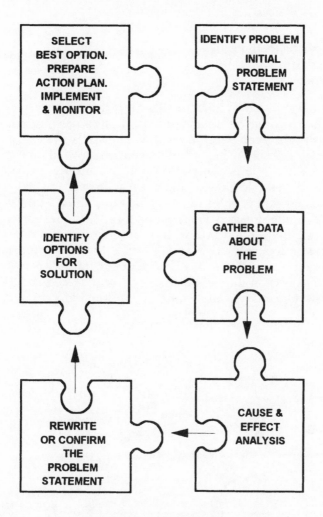

Figure 8.5 *The steps of problem-solving.*

Limit sampling to relevant data only and review any available historical data.

Identifying the real cause of the problem

Cause and effect analysis is a powerful tool for project work. It is easy to use and focuses everyone on a wide range of possible causes. The Ishikawa or 'fishbone' diagram is developed by examining all the possible causes under the four headings:

- people;
- process or method;
- materials;
- equipment.

An example is given in Figure 8.6. Start the diagram by drawing a large box on the right-hand side of a large piece of paper and writing the observed effect in the box. Then draw a horizontal line out to the left from the box across the paper. Now add four arrows, one for each of the headings from which causes are expected to come. Add possible causes under each heading to the relevant arrow to develop a wide range of possible causes of the effects observed. Some causes will appear on more than one arrow but do not restrict them if you believe they are relevant.

When you feel you have enough causes to work with, eliminate any obvious causes you are confident are false. Then look for repeated causes on different arrows and link these together. These are possibly primary causes and you can then identify secondary causes.

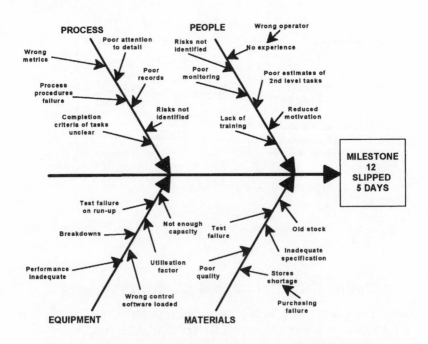

Figure 8.6 *Example of a 'fishbone diagram'.*

Rewrite the problem statement

After analysis review the problem statement and rewrite if appropriate, adding the causes identified:

'The problem is ... which we believe to be caused by ...'

This statement should now clearly identify the real problem with the probable causes and is the basis for seeking a solution.

Seeking a solution

Solutions to problems don't just appear. They are based on a mixture of opinion, historical experience and facts available. Collect the team together and use brainstorming to derive possible ways to resolve the problem. Remember to observe the basic rules:

- write down everything said regardless how apparently stupid;
- suspend all judgement and criticism;
- seek quantity not quality.

When the list of ideas is significant, eliminate duplicates and obvious non-starters and then agree the list of possible solutions. Try to get three options as possible solutions to the problem and check the consequences of applying each. You must seek the 'best' option under the prevailing circumstances, based on cost, resource implications and effects on the schedule.

Implement the selected option

Develop an action plan to implement the agreed solution and confirm responsibilities are clearly defined. Use the steps in Checklist 20 for action planning. Then take the decision and monitor that the outcomes are the same as expected.

PROGRESS MEETINGS

Regular progress meetings are an essential part of the project control process. These meetings can take a considerable amount of time if you do not take specific actions to make them effective. Project progress meetings are not an opportunity for ego-boosting with a huge display of technical ability. All the good things that have happened before the meeting are good news, but ancient history. You want to know about the bad things that have happened which you do not yet know about:

- tasks that have slipped;
- resource conflict problems;
- equipment failures or absence;
- materials not available;
- milestones slipping;
- technical difficulties.

Remember that time spent in a meeting is time lost to project work, so keep your meetings to the point, avoiding diversions and strictly timed. Effective meetings only come from good control by the leader. Try and develop a standard agenda and always have an

Item No.	Action to take	By: whom	Date to finish

Figure 8.7 *Prepare an action list on flip chart sheets.*

CHECKLIST 21:
PROJECT PROGRESS MEETINGS

Always have a timed agenda and keep them short.
Set the start and finish time – and stick to them.

Ask questions to identify:

- What has been completed on time?
- Any outstanding exceptions to the work done?
- What actions agreed earlier are incomplete?
- When outstanding action plans will be complete?
- Which milestones are completed on time?
- Which milestones have slipped?
- Whether action plans are in place to correct slippages?
- Any risks escalated to issues?
- Issues still waiting to be resolved?
- Any resource capacity changes forecast?
- What work is to be done in the next period?
- Which milestones are due in the next period?
- What problems are anticipated in the next period?
- Any risks that could affect the work in the next period?
- Any problems anticipated with third-party contracts in the next period?
- Any team performance problems and issues?

Encourage ideas and suggestions from the team but avoid:

- long verbal reports of what has been done;
- problem-solving in the meeting – set up a separate meeting to resolve problems;
- long debates – they detract from the purpose and cause deviation;
- negotiations – usually excludes most of those present;
- 'any other business' – the biggest timewaster!

---

updated version of the key stage Gantt chart available for reference. Identify the outstanding issues but do not try to solve them in the meeting – set up a separate discussion with the relevant people.

Always have a flip chart stand in the meeting room and record agreed actions on the sheet as they occur with responsibility and target completion date as in Figure 8.7. In this way there should be no doubt in the team who is responsible for which actions and they do not have to wait for the minutes. The *action list* is the most

---

important document to come out of the meeting and this is the starting point of the next meeting – checking that all previous actions are completed.

Yesterday is history – you can't turn the clock back. Focus the team on what must be done next.

PROGRESS REPORTING

At the launch of the project you decided the reporting and communication processes to use (see Chapter 7 for a reminder). Throughout the execution phase of the project check these processes are working and providing the right information for effective control. If the methods are not working well then agree with the team how to improve them. Do not put this off until later or the next project. Continuous improvement is important so grasp any opportunity to do the job better.

Check with your customer and the project sponsor that they are getting all the essential information in the reporting process. You do not want to spend all your time preparing reports so do make sure the process provides essential data only and avoids creating an enormous paper trail. It is very easy to generate large volumes of paper, particularly using computers, and most of this information is never read. Keep reports short using templates, but expect to make a more detailed presentation at a full project review.

Project control is dependent on good communication and it is your obligation to keep the process working always to avoid confusion and misunderstandings.

Project records

It is essential to maintain accurate project records and encourage everyone involved to accept this obligation from the outset. Write everything down to remember! The project file is a source of all relevant information, current and historical, about the project and must be comprehensively maintained. This includes all latest issues of standardised records including those held on computer systems. Do not rely on the integrity or availability of computer records alone. The information in the file includes at least:

- the stakeholder list;
- the project organisation chart;
- the project brief;
- the scope of work statement;
- the project risk log;
- risk management forms;
- the plan schedules and all updates;
- estimating records;
- key stage responsibility charts;
- activity responsibility charts;
- the issue log if you decide to use one;
- issue management forms;
- the project milestone schedule;
- status reports;
- meetings minutes/action lists;
- project change requests;
- project review reports;
- contracts;
- financial reports and documentation;
- customer and supplier information;
- handover checklist;
- completion certificate(s);
- evaluation report.

Remember the project file is a living record of the project and becomes an invaluable source of data for future projects.

The project log book

If you opened a project log book at the start of the project, use it as a daily diary of events in the project. Always keep it with you and record events as they happen. The information you note here will help during the evaluation process after handover to the customer.

PROJECTS AND CONFLICT

Your project involves many individuals and groups of people. The hopes, desires and needs of these people are often incompatible with each other and these differences lead to conflict. When such differences surface they are often seen as difficult, troublesome, annoying or even embarrassing and an intrusion into a calm and ordered life. Conflict and change are partners, never far apart, so accept the inevitable and be prepared to react when necessary.

A large part of your time can be occupied with fighting the fires and crises evolving from conflicts. Many conflicts occur from situations where roles and responsibilities are not clearly defined leaving the team members confused.

Why does conflict occur?

Although many reasons for conflict are quoted some common causes are:

- diverse expertise in the project team;
- low level of authority given to the project leader;
- lack of understanding of the project objectives by the project team;
- excessive role ambiguity in the team – unclear or shared responsibilities;
- unclear schedules and performance targets for team members;
- infringement of functional status and roles by project processes and procedures;
- remote functional groups operating almost independently on project work;
- local interference from high level management involvement;
- people don't like each other or don't get on together in their work.

Most conflict arises from the way people behave with each other in a particular situation, and unfortunately behaviour is not predictable. You need all your skills as a leader to resolve a conflict and identify whether it is good or bad for the project.

Conflict is good if it:

- brings problems and issues out into the open for discussion;
- brings the team together, increasing loyalty;
- promotes creativity, generating new ideas and work practices;
- focuses people to give their work more detailed analysis.

Good conflict generates a win–win relationship between individuals, promoting sharing of information and improved motivation.

Bad conflict:

- creates stress, stirring up negative feelings;
- makes the working environment less pleasant;

- severely reduces the effectiveness of communication processes;
- interferes with coordination of effort between groups and individuals;
- encourages an autocratic approach to working.

Bad conflict tends towards a win–lose relationship developing between individuals. In practice there is a spectrum of conflict between the two extremes of good and bad. You need to create a climate in the team where conflict is seen as healthy and valued for the results created. A team with no conflict could be perceived as complacent and lethargic with little creativity.

Types of conflict

The most common types involve one or more of the following:

- resources;
- equipment and facilities;
- budgets and costs;
- technical opinions and trade-offs;
- priorities;
- procedures;
- scheduling and estimating;
- responsibilities;
- personality clashes.

Personality conflicts are often the most difficult to resolve and may only be resolved finally by total separation of the parties.

Conflicts and risks

Many of the conflicts that occur can be predicted as potential events in a preliminary risk assessment. Resource allocation and prioritisation between several active projects or other operational work is frequently a source of conflict, particularly as priorities are changed to satisfy external pressures. Examples of risks that can become a source of conflict include:

- unclear objectives and project definition;
- project priorities versus other work not exposed;
- resources not available when promised;
- delays in interfaces with other projects downstream;
- changes in the scope of work and project parameters;
- technical disagreements in innovation.

Conflict is a behaviour that restricts the project achieving the expectations of the stakeholders. When it occurs conflict must be regarded as an issue to be resolved as quickly as possible to avoid serious consequences.

Managing conflict

Any temporary management situation produces conflicts. This naturally results from the differences in the organisational behaviour of the individuals involved who all come from different functional groups. You have a different view of the work and its priority to the functional manager (of your team members) who takes on the role of resource manager for all the project activity that has to be supported.

You operate in an environment of constant and rapid change. The functional manager works in a more standardised and predictable environment. You have to bridge the gap between these two environments to achieve success.

There is no single method of managing all conflicts in such temporary situations. The real skill is to:

- anticipate their occurrence;
- understand their composition;
- assess the consequences.

Project activity involves people and it is their behaviour that directly contributes to conflict. Constantly look for possible areas of conflict in the same way as project risks are regularly reviewed.

Handling conflict

Everyone has a preferred behaviour in any particular situation that influences how a conflict is approached.

Typically the modes for handling conflict are:

- *Withdrawal* – taking a retreat course: withdrawing from a potential collision course towards what appears to be a disagreement and hoping it will go away on its own.
- *Smoothing* – seeking to establish and then emphasise the areas of agreement and avoiding the areas of disagreement initially, in the hope that the latter can be reduced to minor status as part of the whole and eventually be subject to compromise.
- *Compromising* – starting from a rigid position on both sides but expressing a willingness to search for a solution: allows both

sides to the conflict to feel they are satisfied with the amount gained as well as the amount lost.

- *Forcing* – exerting an opinion or view at the expense of the other: characterised by competitiveness this leads to a win–lose result that ultimately becomes a lose–lose result due to the damaged relationship.
- *Confrontation* – facing the conflict directly to cause face-to-face debate and discussion of the disagreements, deriving options for resolution: often defuses a violent situation and reduces the conflict to a level where compromising or even smoothing can resolve the conflict.

In most conflict situations, you will work with confrontation, compromise and smoothing to resolve conflict in the team or between teams and functions. In dealing with management compromise is the most likely mode but behaviour is influenced by your leadership style.

Resolving conflict is a real test of your ability to negotiate and influence others. You can achieve a successful outcome if you can focus the parties in conflict to identify and agree:

- the areas of full agreement;
- the areas of disagreement.

Then you can use the positive feelings about the areas of agreement to discuss the areas of disagreement one by one in a positive manner. Start with what appears to be the easiest to resolve and work through the list. Expect to fail with some but if you can move the parties concerned to agree on a majority of points it takes the heat out of the remainder.

Effective conflict resolution is dependent on persuading everyone involved to listen to understand, not to evaluate and criticise.

MANAGING TIME

Your primary objective in project work is to achieve a successful outcome which is generally interpreted as delivering the right results on time and to a pre-defined budget. Although this may require you to make changes to the technical elements of the scope and results required, the whole process is dependent on time. As time always moves inexorably on it is common to assume things are happening according to the plans you spend much time developing. The reality is often far from expectations and this is not just because the plans are wrong. Many of the difficulties you will encounter in managing a project are caused by time management going out of control. Some people are very skilled at organising and managing how they use time effectively. Unfortunately many are not so organised and their work output is extremely vulnerable with poor time management.

You are now thinking: 'What has this got to do with me?' A valid question to ask but the answer is that it has everything to do with you. Remember you are responsible for managing performance. Performance is directly related to effort which yields an output and these results are dependent on how well an individual makes the best use of time. So you have a direct interest in how everyone working on even the smallest part of your project is using the time allocated to the actual work. If you have an interest then you can influence how time is used, avoiding unnecessary work, duplication of effort and ensure attention is given to prioritising the work. Time is your most valuable resource which, if lost or misplaced, is gone forever. For you it is therefore a constraint and you must demonstrate and encourage everyone involved to use effective time management principles to maximise this resource.

A large number of projects are seriously understaffed, senior management believing (or hoping) that you will assume the additional workload created by the resource constraint. Unfortunately this is usually easier said than done since you are probably already burdened with other activities of an operational nature as well as possibly other projects! You do manage to cope with this burden of work, often working long hours believing this is the only way to keep control of the project. The most significant problem with people and time management is actually recognising and accepting that there is a problem. The problem can then be regarded as an opportunity to develop effectiveness, reduce the stress and improve the probability of success for your project.

Ask yourself some questions:

- Do you have trouble completing work to deadlines?
- How long can you work at your desk before being interrupted?
- How long can you work at your desk before interrupting yourself?
- How many interruptions (typically) occur each day?
- Have you a procedure for handling interruptions?

- Can you set aside a large block of time for something important?
- How much overtime do you work to get the job done?
- How is incoming mail handled?
- How much time do you spend attending meetings?
- How tough is it to say no?
- Do you carry out work you could allocate to team members?
- Do you make a fresh 'To-Do List' every day?
- Is your list prioritised?
- How do you approach detailed work when it is necessary?
- Do you have flexibility in your diary for reactive time?
- Is your routine work made easier with established procedures?
- Does the team understand your time management principles?

Converting time from a constraint to a manageable resource requires you to work towards dealing with the impact of the above questions. As you are almost certainly doing some of the project work yourself the barriers to effective time management affect you just the same as your team members.

Barriers to effective time management

If you spend too much time doing project work yourself then the consequence is a serious impact of all those things that rob you of valuable time to control the project. If you are unable to say no you quickly become burdened with everyone's problems and the decisions needed to keep the project moving at every level. Many things can rob you of time, including:

- poor communication
- unclear responsibility and authority
- uncontrolled visitors and phone calls
- lack of information
- too many meetings
- too many project reviews
- casual conversations in office
- tracing data and information
- record keeping
- changing priorities
- unclear objectives and project scope
- lack of support and commitment from others
- lack of project tools
- confirming resource commitments
- bureaucracy
- politics and power games
- strong functional boundaries
- arson – running from crisis to crisis
- excessive paperwork

- changes without explanation
- unnecessary crisis interventions
- procrastination
- executive interference
- too much attention to detail
- overcommitment to non-project activities
- coaching inexperienced team members
- inability to assess and take risks
- desire for absolute perfection
- lack of clear organisation
- unclear budget and financial controls
- lack of business strategy

You can probably think of many more, all influencing you to some degree and many having a serious impact on your effectiveness. The consequence of these robbers of time is a reduction in the working day for you and your team. The productive output for most people is about 80 per cent of the available time or everyone really only works a four-day week. If you want proof, try completing a time log sheet for a week, recording what you are doing every 15 or 30 minutes of the day. Review the findings at the end of the week – you may learn something about yourself!

What can you do?

Start by addressing some fundamental issues. You cannot hope to encourage others in your team to improve their time management if you display all the symptoms of hopeless disorganisation. Use your time effectively by:

- Allocating work clearly to the team members.
- Delegating some of your authority where and when appropriate.
- Controlling your own assigned work to the project schedule.
- Not taking on more than you really know you can complete on time.
- Consulting as required, but taking decisions promptly and explaining them.
- Preparing your own 'To-Do List' and *updating every day*.
- Setting your own priorities and generally sticking to them.
- Focusing on the areas of high risk in the currently active project work.
- Doing the difficult tasks first or when you can concentrate most effectively.
- Avoiding unnecessary memos.
- Refusing to do the low importance stuff.

- Controlling the time on the telephone – using a block of time for several calls together.
- Controlling the project work by exception, reviewing the plan charts each day.
- Setting out a fixed agenda for project meetings.
- Not holding meetings for the sake of getting together – having a clear purpose.
- Avoiding wanderlust – monitoring effectively when necessary.
- Focusing everyone on the project objectives.
- Showing your concern for success.
- Turning problems into opportunities to progress and learn.

Regularly ask yourself some simple questions:

- What am I doing that really does not need doing?
- What am I doing that someone else could do just as well or even better than me?
- What am I not doing that will not get done anyway if I avoid doing it?
- What have I done to establish clear priorities and targets for me and my team?
- Have I confirmed that everyone clearly understands what is expected of them?
- Have I communicated the current priorities to everyone who needs to know?
- Does everyone know and understand the consequences of ignoring the priorities?
- Is everyone aware of the high risk areas and the triggers to identify potential issues?

The answers will lead you to improve the way you use time and encourage others to adopt the same process. Review your performance at the end of each day and give yourself a reward if you consider you are improving.

Working in a matrix

Or is it 'working in a maze?', because that is how it feels sometimes. It is easy to be pulled in two or more directions at once, each promising a satisfactory conclusion. Most of the projects in an organisation are carried out using people in different departments, divisions or even on different sites and countries. How can you possibly hope to manage the team member's effective use of time and maintain your project schedule in such an environment?

The short answer is with 'great difficulty and a risk of increased stress levels', although there are some actions you can take to help make everyone's life more comfortable.

- Keep the stakeholder list up to date, particularly with the line managers of all the resources you are using or plan to use in the future. These people control the time these resources can give your project and hold the keys to success. Your ability to influence them will be continually tested to ensure the project work is always started and completed on time. Keep them well informed of the project progress and agree with them how the work is to be broken down into reasonable chunks for effectiveness. Remind them of the consequences to the business if the project suffers a slippage.
- One of the most significant timewasters in project work is the effect of 'back-tracking'. When the project file is opened to start a piece of work there is inevitably a need to review what happened the last time some work was done. If that was several days before, then there is a need to go back over what was done and achieved. The time for this 'back-track' is often significant, especially when you add up the number of times it happens in a project where people are only doing your work at intervals amongst other activities. Add up the total time used in this way in a project and it is almost frightening. The consequences of going back over previous work may cause a complete review and amendment of earlier work which might be beneficial occasionally but is often unnecessary rework.
- Try to get agreement that project work is always given a sufficiently large chunk of time to achieve some specific measurable output without any interruptions. Changes of priority are inevitable in departments you do not control and putting out the fires in operational areas of the business are essential activities. But fires are often encouraged or even lit for political reasons and you must try and get line managers to enter into firm commitments that your work will not suffer unnecessarily. It is often an excuse for lack of progress.
- Encourage your team members to work out their own time priorities, giving support and guidance when appropriate. Agree the time allocated to your project work and satisfy yourself that it is adequate to complete the work on time.

Remember everyone is different in the way they work and their pace. Encourage the team to expose and discuss their project work priorities with their line manager so that interruptions can be minimised and time used effectively. This helps line managers to control and map their departmental resource utilisation.

- With the agreement of the line manager of each resource, set out personal targets for each member of the team. These are effectively the dates created in the project plan, but changes are often caused by the changing priorities and minor slippages of earlier work. You must continually review these targets and take into account the slippages and the actions implemented to correct the time lost. The plan is dynamic and must be regularly updated for these changes and distributed to everyone involved.

- Do not allow slippages to go unreported to you and the line manager with missed targets, pushing your project into fire-fighting mode. Try and keep proactive, continually monitoring future resource loadings and commitments so you can assess the impact on your project. This will minimise the incidence of unforeseen risks and you can use 'what-if' analysis with the Gantt Chart to decide corrective actions to keep everything on track.

The most significant cause of failure in a matrix type project is poor communication. This causes major chunks of time to be lost through misunderstandings. These are usually due to poor listening and unclear communications with little or poor back-up documentation. Use the milestone schedule as a means of communicating to everyone the key dates which must not be missed and check that everyone understands their obligations to meet these dates. Keep the responsibility charts updated and re-issued and insist that you need to know immediately if there is any doubt or lack of clarity by anyone about what is necessary or expected to meet those milestones on time.

The 'feudal kingdoms'

The hierarchical organisational structure that is familiar to everyone is a perfect arrangement for the development of little empires within the organisation. The consequent departmental empires become a collection of kingdoms each with their baron who has total authority over the constituent manors or sections. This structural system from the 9th century still exists in some contemporary organisations where departments have containing walls which can only be breached if you follow specific unwritten rules. This creates an organisation with little integration where the departmental heads set their own rules and norms, making cross-functional coordinated working extremely difficult. Power games and political machinations occupy much management time and each is suspicious of the next with a high level of protectionism. Comments like 'We don't do things that way round here,' are common and consistent working practices such as those needed for project work are regarded with considerable mistrust. It is almost like a war zone with missiles thrown at regular intervals to keep the 'enemy' at length, and avoid being blamed when anything goes wrong.

This may sound like an extreme situation but to various degrees it does exist too much today in many organisations. Projects identified as strategic and cross-functional have little real chance of success in such an environment. There are too many opportunities for individuals to attack and sabotage the efforts of a project team. Breaking down the walls or barriers to create an environment for successful cooperation with a common vision is clearly a task for the senior management of the organisation. They must want to create an open environment where everyone is clearly focused on a strategic vision.

The consequences for your project are serious when a feudal kingdom is encountered. You find it impossible to reach agreements or even if you do they are frequently ignored and broken. There is little sense of obligation demonstrated by the baron or lords of the manors and any attempt to create a real sense of good time management is hopeless. Your only course of action is to take the difficulties directly to your project sponsor with clearly illustrated evidence of the impact on the project. A strategic project should have a *must not fail* label which all departmental managers must acknowledge and your sponsor has the authority to cross the boundaries of these empires and create an atmosphere of willing cooperation.

Your project is always vulnerable and all your efforts to encourage good time management and keep the project on track are wasted unless you respond promptly to such issues and escalate them for some very prompt action.

Have regular 1:1's

Many of the time management problems can be reduced and their impact reduced with quick identification and realisation that there is a problem. Performance management is an essential part of your job and this needs regular contact with all your resources and the stakeholders, particularly if the latter have responsibility for some of the actual project work. The 1:1 meetings with each team member are essential to help you:

- demonstrate your concern and interest in their welfare
- understand the individual person
- learn about their experience, skills, interests, beliefs, and aspirations
- learn how they feel about their work
- discover what concerns they have about their work
- learn what problems they have with the work itself
- discover what difficulties they have with managing their time effectively
- agree personal targets aligned to the plan
- monitor and discuss performance
- identify areas for future training and development
- agree any relevant recommendations to pass to their line manager.

The meetings are meant to be informal but actions agreed are recorded and reviewed in the next discussion. Allow 30–45 minutes for each meeting and decide a frequency at the start of the project. Usually a monthly dialogue of this type is adequate but it does depend on the length of the project. Diarised monthly discussions of this type never prevent ad-hoc discussions and do not take the place of regular monitoring activities.

Your team members are giving a part of their available capacity to your work. In many situations their own line managers will not have much contact with them during this work, beyond some general concerns for their welfare. You have close and detailed information about each team member's performance and this needs to pass back to their line manager as part of the more formalised performance appraisal process. You can only make an objective contribution to this process through having a regular dialogue with each team member. A subsequent poor or indifferent appraisal review interview may be blamed on you with quite serious impact on an individual's motivation!

CHECKLIST 22:
ENCOURAGE GOOD TIME MANAGEMENT

Self

- Identify your own time management problems.
- Regard time as a manageable resource, not a constraint.
- Focus on priorities, short- and medium-term.
- Create effective procedures and adopt them as a habit.
- Identify the barriers and time robbers that affect your work.
- Derive action plan to eliminate the time robbers.
- Review your progress at regular intervals.

The team

- Have regular 1:1's to discuss performance.
- Encourage good time management practices.
- Support and give guidance where appropriate.
- Encourage self-evaluation and measurement of improvement.
- Create an open atmosphere where time problems are discussed.

Stakeholders

- Keep up to date with progress and changes.
- Agree acceptable breakdown of the work avoiding too many small chunks.
- Eliminate the opportunities for excessive 'back-tracking'.
- Keep the focus on the project objectives and strategic priority.
- React promptly to structural barriers hindering the work.
- Escalate cooperation issues promptly to the project sponsor.
- Have regular 1:1's with your sponsor.

Remember that you need a similar regular dialogue with your project sponsor to sustain your own motivation to achieve success.

CONTROLLING THE PROJECT COSTS

The control of expenditure is important to all organisations, yet many do not measure and monitor the costs of their business projects. The highest proportion of these costs is frequently associated with the resources used and this is regarded as part of the operating costs of the business. Control of your project is not just about controlling the effort and work outputs, but should involve cost measurement. It is not just the domain of the finance department. You are keen to demonstrate success and this is only total if you do not exceed the budget.

The data for setting up a budget and gathering expenditure information exists in every management information system. Often the projects have a low priority with finance people, who are mainly concerned to produce business operating statements rapidly each month. In many organisations the only way you can have accurate and up-to-date information on how much you have spent is to do it yourself. Once you make a commitment to spend some money in your project, it is out of your budget. The finance report may still not record this commitment until an invoice appears several weeks or months later. The budget report still shows you have more money left than is really true!

Of course cost control is only effective if *all* costs are measured, including the costs of people working on the project. This means everyone must record their time spent on project work so that this can be costed with cost rates derived by the finance people. Cost rates often include all indirect costs such as rents, heating, lighting, etc for the organisation. If the time data is not collected in a consistent and disciplined way, then you cannot control the costs accurately. Your monitoring process must therefore include accurate measurement of:

- the time spent on each task;
- the resources used on all tasks;
- cost of materials (and wastage) used;
- cost of equipment time used;
- capital expenditure committed;
- revenue expenditure committed.

Normally you make these measurements over a specific period of two or four weeks or by calendar month.

For effective control you need information on:

- the project budget, a cumulative total divided into accounting periods;
- the costs incurred in the current accounting period;
- the costs incurred to date from the start;
- the work scheduled for completion according to the plan in the current period;
- the total work scheduled for completion to date;
- the work actually completed in the current period;
- the total work actually completed to date.

You can use the WBS and the key stage Gantt chart as the basis of collecting this data.

Cost control measures

Four essential measures are used for the control of project costs.

1. BAC – Budget at completion

This is based on the operating budget developed from the WBS for the whole project.

2. BCWS – Budgeted cost of the work scheduled

At any specific time the schedule shows a certain amount of work should be completed. This is presented as a percentage completion of the total work of the project at that time. Then:

$$\% \text{ scheduled completion} \times \text{BAC} = \text{BCWS}$$

3. BCWP – Budgeted cost of the work performed

At any specified time the actual work measured as complete is compared with the scheduled amount and the real percentage completion calculated. Then:

$$\% \text{ actual completion} \times \text{BAC} = \text{BCWP}$$

The BCWP is known as the *earned value* of the work completed.

4. ACWP – Actual cost of work performed

At any specified time the actual cost incurred for the work. The timing of the actual cost measurement coincides with the percentage completion progress measurement so that the actual cost can be compared with earned value (BCWP).

Other terms often used include:

5. FTC – Forecast to completion

A forecast of the cost to be incurred to complete the remaining work. This may be an extrapolation using an analysis model or simply the costs to date added to your best estimates of all the costs to complete the project.

6. CV – Cost variance

The difference between the value of the work performed and the actual cost for that work, ie:

$$CV = BCWP - ACWP$$

If the actual cost is above budget the CV becomes negative!

7. SV – Schedule variance

The difference between the value of the work performed and the value of the work that had been scheduled to be performed, at the same measurement point in time, ie:

$$SV = BCWP - BCWS$$

If the work done is behind schedule the SV becomes negative!

The variance measures are often used for trend analysis, because of their sensitivity to changes as the project progresses.

It's the costs that run away – and the legacy of cost overruns lasts longer than the project itself!

The cost control diagram

A convenient way to show the relationships between the cost measures in a graphic format is known as the *cost control diagram*. The ACWP and BCWP curves in Figure 8.8 are exaggerated to show the relationships clearly. In practice both measures tend to cycle with time both above and below the budget curve (BCWS) and a mean curve is drawn through the scatter of points. The most accurate way is to tabulate all data using a spreadsheet program on a computer to calculate and update the data at regular intervals.

Using a spreadsheet on a computer makes it easier to incorporate any amendments to the budget resulting from major changes to the project. Most spreadsheets include charting features and the data is then used to automatically generate the diagram for each reporting period.

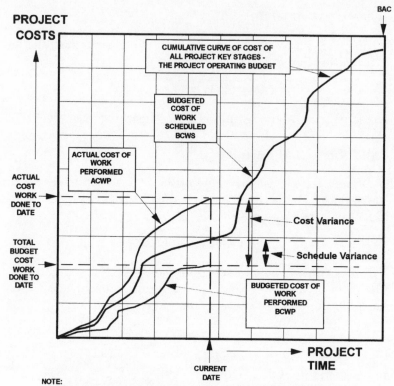

Figure 8.8 *The cost control diagram.*

SUMMARY

Figure 8.9 summarises the key steps you repeatedly go through during project execution. Checklist 23 identifies some key leadership actions during this phase.

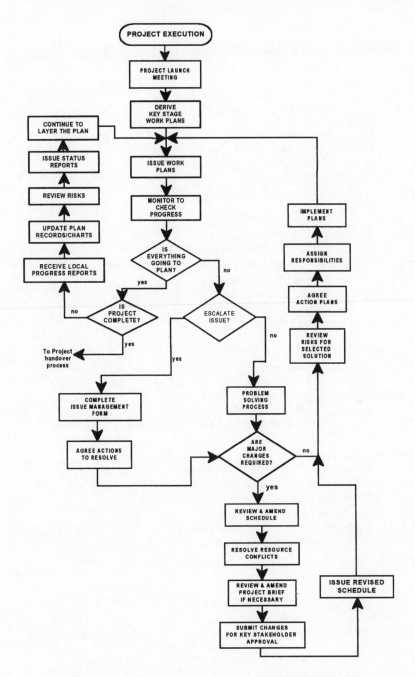

Figure 8.9 *Process flow diagram — Project execution.*

CHECKLIST 23: KEY LEADERSHIP ACTIONS DURING PROJECT EXECUTION

■ *The stakeholders:*
- Report progress regularly.
- Involve in problem-solving.
- Maintain commitment with regular contact.
- Encourage feedback of changing needs.
- Regulate plan changes.
- Seek approval of major changes.

■ *Project tasks:*
- Confirm resource commitments.
- Continue to layer the plan detail.
- Derive and sign off work plans as work progresses.
- Modify plan as appropriate.
- Review progress against project brief.
- Track and record progress against plan baseline.
- Keep updated records of all cost information.

■ *Team members:*
- Coordinate teamworking.
- Encourage participation of extended team members.
- Involve everyone in replanning activities.
- Resolve conflict and issues promptly.
- Actively support team efforts with guidance and assistance.

■ *Team members:*
- Advise and coach when opportune.
- Hold regular one-to-one meetings to discuss performance.
- Stress priorities.
- Recognise and praise effort.
- Encourage participation in teamwork.
- React positively to performance issues.

9

CLOSING YOUR PROJECT

All good things must end – even your project! You have diligently nursed your project through the earlier phases and experienced the excitement of achieving the desired deliverables. You have over-come the trials and tribulations of the issues that seemed like 'Mission Impossible' at the time to emerge within sight of the finishing line. This final phase of your project still has all the potential for success or failure. Many issues can still occur and you must continue to monitor carefully to ensure a successful outcome. Closure of a project does not happen, you must plan it with care.

As the project approaches the end it is easy for senior manage-ment to appear to lose interest. They are looking ahead to the next project and this can be perceived as a lack of commitment. Your communication processes must keep them involved right up to the celebration of completion. The last thing you want is to become infected with a common virus – 'project drift'.

Project drift

This occurs when you let the pressure off the control system as the end approaches. It is easy for the customer or any stakeholder to throw in a few add-ons: 'Just before you finish the project will you have a look at this modification?' This is the first sounding of the death knell! Control of late changes of mind adds significant extra work just as you are tidying up to prepare for handover to the customer. These extras are not budgeted, can add considerable costs to the project and seriously affect the schedule. Any sig-nificant changes at this stage are best treated as a follow-on project after closing the current project.

There is also another consequence of add-ons – the motivation of your team. You are concerned about what happens next and so are the members of your team. They are concerned about their next assignment and this may show as a reduced motivation. The impact on remaining tasks is a possible slowing down of effort and lack of commitment. You must keep the momentum going and avoid losing team members to other projects or operational activities.

Similarly your customer may suffer such effects and not bother to attend meetings so readily. The users will be anticipating the handover and may attempt to advance the completion taking shortcuts. If the changes the users have to accept at handover are still not popular or accepted, they may obstruct completion and create additional work to cause delays. All these difficulties can be anticipated if you have maintained effective communication and involve the stakeholders closely in the closure process.

Establish completion criteria

Agree with your customer and their user group just what completion means to them. Identify the specific criteria they want to use to confirm completion.

Project completion is signified by:

- all tasks finished;
- specific deliverables finished;
- testing programmes finished;
- training programmes prepared and/or finished;
- equipment installed and operating;
- documentation manuals finished;
- process procedures finished and tested;
- staff training finished.

All criteria for completion must be measurable by agreed methods or conflict will be inevitable.

One of the key stages in your plan should be the acceptance process for handover to your customer. Your ultimate objective is to delight your customer so validate the acceptance process now.

THE ACCEPTANCE PROCESS

For most projects it is easy for the team to identify the essential steps of handover. The acceptance process is based on a checklist you must agree with your customer and the user group. This checklist includes a list of activities that must be finished before acceptance is confirmed. The list includes questions on various topics depending on the type of project:

- unfinished non-critical work;
- the project tasks – based on the WBS;
- the deliverables achieved – based on the project brief;
- quality standards attained – based on the scope of work statement;
- supply of equipment;
- installation of equipment;
- testing and validation of equipment;
- testing and validation of operating processes;
- documentation manuals;
- new standard operating procedures;
- design of training programmes;
- training of operating staff and management;
- training of maintenance staff;
- setting up a help desk;
- establishing a maintenance function;
- outstanding issues awaiting resolution;
- identifying follow-on projects;
- limits of acceptability.

The acceptance process should also identify the customer representative who has the authority to sign the project completion report.

In addition confirm:

- who is responsible for each step of the acceptance process and the work involved;
- what post-project support is required and who is responsible;
- what post-project support can be available;
- for how long such support must be given.

Once an agreed process is produced with a handover checklist you are ready to implement the final stages of the project. You can then set up the *close-out meeting*.

THE CLOSE-OUT MEETING

Prepare the team well for this important meeting. It is the culmination of all your efforts over many weeks or months.

Hold a team meeting to review:

- the project WBS;
- the project brief;
- the key stage Gantt chart;
- the project risk log;
- the project issue log;
- the final key stage work plan charts;
- the project milestone schedule.

Check that all work is finishing on time and no forgotten tasks are expected. At this stage it is quite common to find a number of outstanding minor tasks from earlier key stages still unfinished. They are not critical and have not impeded progress, yet they must be completed. Set clear targets in this final sweep to complete all these tasks soon to avoid giving your customer an excuse to withhold acceptance.

Then go through the handover checklist agreed with your customer and set targets for the team for any outstanding work to complete. Focus on outstanding issues and allocate responsibility for each with clear target dates for resolution. When you are satisfied that everything is under control confirm the date of the close-out meeting with your customer and the project sponsor.

At this meeting you:

- review the project results achieved;
- go through the handover checklist;
- confirm and explain action plans for any outstanding work to tidy up;
- confirm and explain action plans for any outstanding issues;
- agree and confirm responsibilities for any ongoing work or support;
- confirm who is responsible for monitoring project benefits;
- present the *completion report* for approval and sign-off;
- thank the team for their efforts;
- thank the stakeholders for their support and commitment;
- thank the customer and your project sponsor for their support and commitment.

Provided you have done everything the handover checklist demands, acceptance should be agreed and the completion report (see Figure 9.1) approved and signed.

You will probably leave this meeting with a feeling of considerable relief – if your project is signed off. But you have not quite finished yet! So delay the final celebrations for a few days because now you must carry out an evaluation of the project.

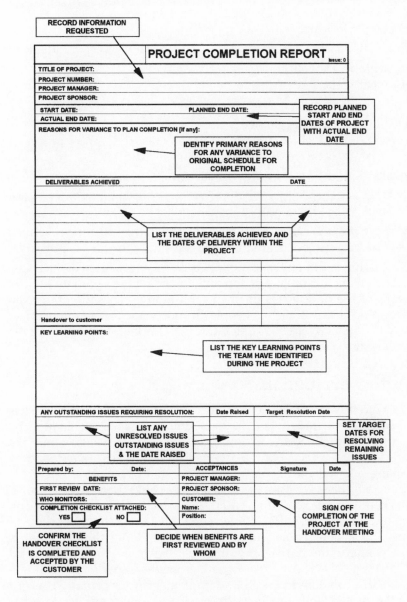

Figure 9.1 *The project completion report.*

EVALUATING YOUR PROJECT

Question: Why evaluate?
Answer: To learn.

Evaluation is the process used to review the project and identify:

- what went well
- what went badly

and then ask: 'Why?'

Question: What is evaluated?
Answer: The technical work, achievements, the project processes and the management of the project.

Evaluation of projects normally has two modes:

- *active* – a continuous process throughout the project life, with occasional specific reviews or 'audits';
- *post-project* – after the project is handed over to your customer. The post-project evaluation provides data for future projects.

Evaluation is difficult to complete because everyone who has been involved in the project is looking to their next assignment. The work of the project has finished with motivation and enthusiasm dropping to a low level. People do not want to be reminded of what went badly and start an inquest at this late stage, viewing the events as ancient history.

Active evaluation

This often happens by default. An effective project team is always keen to learn from what they are doing. Promote evaluation by encouraging the team to question the way they carry out the project work. This is particularly valid when issues are resolved by asking relevant questions. When you ask an open question about an event, there are always consequential questions that follow.

There are no rules for evaluation, just let the team focus on identifying opportunities for learning. This is continuous improvement in action leading to better ways of doing things. What is more important is that anything learned must be accepted and broadcast so everyone can benefit from the experience. This is a more difficult activity for you to implement. Your primary concern is the project and you have little time to spend talking to other project managers about events that have occurred and how they were resolved. They may only show a passing casual interest since they are similarly focused on their projects.

Suggest to your project sponsor that a forum of project managers meet occasionally to share learning from their project activities. Particularly important events and the resulting improvements in project process could be the subject of a special presentation. An alternative approach is to start a project newsletter for your project community. This has the additional benefit of giving publicity and recognition to particular projects, project teams and the results achieved. The newsletter takes some of the mystery and secrecy out of the organisation's project activities.

CHECKLIST 24: ACTIVE EVALUATION

For any event, ask:

- Why did this happen?
- What were the consequences?
- Was it good or bad for the project, stakeholders, team?
- Could the situation have been anticipated?
- Were there early signals that went unrecognised at the time?
- When was the situation first identified?
- Who should have reacted?
- Was it due to unclear responsibility or authority?
- Was it due to poor estimating?
- Was it due to poor planning?
- Has there been a failure of any stakeholder to fulfil their obligations?
- Has there been a communication failure?
- Where have our communication processes failed?
- Can we correct these failures now?
- Has the control system failed us?
- Is the event a direct result of current organisational policies?
- What have we learned from the event(s)?
- What changes can we implement now to prevent a recurrence?
- Are policy changes necessary?
- Are the learning points valuable for other project teams?
- How can we check the learning points are communicated now?

Post-project evaluation

Valuable experience and information are gained during a project. Much of this is lost in project archives and never recovered to help future project teams. You and your team members will remember the highlights. As you all move on to other activities and projects, the learning points become dimmed with the passage of time. Lessons learned during a project should be documented and distributed to individuals engaged or likely to be engaged in project activities. Opportunities for improving processes and procedures are continually present. Some of the learning from projects should be incorporated into the organisation's policy.

It is appropriate to carry out post-project evaluation asking in-depth and searching questions about each dimension of the project manager's role:

- managing the project stakeholders;
- managing the project lifecycle;
- managing performance of the stakeholders, yourself and the team.

In all areas when questions are asked there are inevitably consequent questions of cause and effect to be answered by the project team as a means of checking all possible learning points are identified. The results of this evaluation should be published in the post-project or post-mortem report. It is easy to avoid the events where things went wrong because of the potential risk of hurting someone's feelings. If it involves senior management it may be perceived as direct criticism and career limiting! Focus on facts, not perceptions and avoid negative statements. Every negative has an equal and opposite positive, so seek the positives that will give the organisation benefits in the future. For example, a statement about the poor performance of a project sponsor can easily be perceived as highly critical. Turn this into a positive statement:

> At week six a slippage of three weeks was incurred due to delays in the approval of the primary plan (*fact*). This was caused by the project sponsor being absent overseas resolving problems on project X (*fact*). The delay could have been avoided if another executive manager or the project manager had been given the necessary authority during this period of absence (*learning*).

Checklist 25 lists some typical questions to ask during the evaluation process. Such a list can never be exhaustive, because many specific questions are directly related to a particular project. Add further questions to ask for your project. Every question yields an answer that generates more questions to ask and you must decide where to stop. Remember the purpose of this whole process is to learn.

Evaluation is not an exercise in self-gratification. The process must be an objective one at all times, not to place blame or boost individual egos.

CHECKLIST 25: POST-PROJECT EVALUATION

Ask questions about the stakeholders:

- Were the needs correctly identified initially?
- Was the project purpose statement correct?
- Did the needs change during the project due to unforeseen events?
- Were the benefits correctly identified and satisfied by the project?
- Were the expected results obtained?
- Were unexpected results obtained?
- Is there a follow-up need to be examined in subsequent projects?
- Were all stakeholders identified at the outset?
- Did new stakeholders appear during the project?
- Were stakeholders managed effectively?
- Did stakeholders interfere unnecessarily with the detail?
- Did any external stakeholders fail in their obligations?

Ask questions about the project lifecycle:

- Was there a feasibility study carried out?
- Who defined the project purpose?
- Was the project manager appointed at the outset?
- Were responsibility, authority and accountability clearly defined for the project manager?
- Were realistic timescales established for the project?
- Were project objectives clear and understood?
- Were all tasks clearly established with accurate durations?
- Was the plan logic correct?
- Were project resources correctly estimated?
- Were work plans for each team member clearly established?
- Were all team members aware of their responsibilities and authority?
- Were all resource commitments honoured?
- Were milestones clearly established?
- Were project review meetings built into the plan?
- Were all resource constraints identified and resolved?
- Were risks identified and regularly monitored?

- Was there a documented control system understood by everyone?
- Were there clear lines of communication for monitoring and providing feedback?
- Did the reporting process work effectively?
- Did project meetings achieve their purpose?
- Were all issues resolved promptly?
- Were all project changes documented and handled promptly?
- How was individual performance measured and communicated?
- Was the budget communicated to everyone?
- Were cost and expenditure information monitored regularly and reported to the team?
- Were the end users satisfied with the results?
- Was the customer involved in the design of an acceptance process?
- Were the team and project manager satisfied with the results?
- Are there follow-up and maintenance activities?
- What actions are required to close the project files?
- What have we all learned from this project that will assist management in future?

Ask questions about performance:

- Did the project sponsor fulfil their obligations?
- Were there delays caused by any stakeholder?
- Did any stakeholder avoid their responsibility?
- Did the team meet regularly?
- Did the team work well together?
- Was individual performance appraised regularly?
- Were failures to meet personal targets subject to investigation?
- Were conflicts and grievances dealt with promptly?
- Did the team and project manager review their performance regularly?
- Have additional training needs been identified as a result of performance assessment?
- Is recognition appropriate?
- What recommendations can be made to improve future performance?

Technical evaluation

The technical evaluation is concerned to demonstrate that the best results were obtained with the skills, experience and technology available to you throughout the project. You need to focus the team to identify where successes were achieved and also where technical problems occurred. The technical work of the project is the principal area where you have endeavoured to encourage the highest creativity from team members. Turning this creativity into innovative results is the underlying objective of the whole project. Much can be learned from how this was done and is fundamental to the growth of knowledge in the organisation.

It is important to recognise that your technical achievements may have a value to others, often far more than you can realise at the current time. Do ensure that the technical part of your evaluation report is distributed to anyone who could benefit from your efforts. This is an essential activity in any organisation with a commitment to grow. The information you gather through evaluation must be shared widely if the organisation is to realise the maximum benefits from your efforts. You will similarly learn from the efforts of your colleagues with other projects.

CHECKLIST 26: TECHNICAL EVALUATION

Typical questions to ask include:

- Were the original objectives technically feasible and realistic?
- Were the customer's needs accurately specified?
- Was the customer accurately presenting the user's requirements?
- Did the technology exist?
- Did new technology have to be developed as part of the project?
- Were the right skills available to develop this new technology?
- Was specialised training necessary for the project?
- Were the products variations or derivatives of existing products?
- Was new equipment required?
- Did new equipment have to be developed?
- Were new test procedures required?
- How were these developed?
- Was specialised test equipment developed?
- How were technical difficulties resolved?
- Were consultants involved?
- Are any new designs and technology protected?
- Can we patent any of the developments?
- What is the confidence level of the technical performance?
- Have additional opportunities for improvements been identified?
- Can any technical developments be used on other projects?
- Are there possibilities identified for other products?
- Has all essential documentation been completed?
- Who else needs to know about the technical results obtained?

POST-PROJECT APPRAISALS

At some stage after the project handover the project benefits should be measured. When you carry out the evaluation the project is complete and the customer has accepted the results. The benefits of the project are not all apparent. Some benefits could come from the project during the execution phase, depending on the type of project.

At the definition phase of the project you set out the project benefits. These are likely to be concerned with:

- generating improvements in equipment and plant performance;
- creating new income from a new product introduction;
- improved efficiency from re-engineering processes and procedures;
- increased effectiveness from skills enhancement by training programmes.

All of these benefits can be quantified and measured by metrics agreed with your customer. If a cost-benefit analysis exists from the project initiation then a forecast exists of the benefits against time. This is often presented as cost savings through the improved efficiencies or increased income, contribution or profitability from the new product introduction.

At the closure of the project, agree who is responsible for the measurement of benefits and when they are to be reviewed. The customer may decide to take this responsibility and release you for the next project. However, the project has produced a successful outcome and you will almost certainly want an involvement even if it only means getting regular reports over the next 12 months. Although you attempt to create a clean handover to the customer you will probably have a continuing contact for a short period as part of the post-project support process.

When the benefits accumulate later, give the team members some feedback – they will be interested.

WHAT NEXT?

You have finished the project, delighted your customer and reported your evaluation in a final report. Now you can celebrate with your team – a job well done! Call a celebration team meeting and ask the customer and other stakeholders to come along. Ask your project sponsor to address the group and put on record the success achieved. After the euphoria of this celebration remember to make sure your project file is completely updated before you close it for the last time! Check that you have taken action on:

- any future responsibilities for the team members;
- reassignments for all the team members;
- identifying any training needs for yourself and team members;
- informing line managers of team members that the project is complete;
- passing on training needs to relevant line managers and the training department;
- thanking the line managers for their support and commitment.

But what does come next? Perhaps another project, promotion or just back to operational activities? Ask yourself what you gained from the experience of managing the project and what actions you can take to improve your performance even more. Every project is unique, involving different people and different skills. Your continued development comes from this self-analysis that will lead you on to greater success in the future. This success is directly related to your commitment. Develop the skills of project management further for the larger projects that are becoming a part of working life in most organisations today.

Project work is enormously rewarding and creates a great sense of achievement.

SUMMARY

Figure 9.2 summarises the key steps of project closure. Checklist 27 identifies the key leadership actions to give particular attention to during this final critical phase of the project.

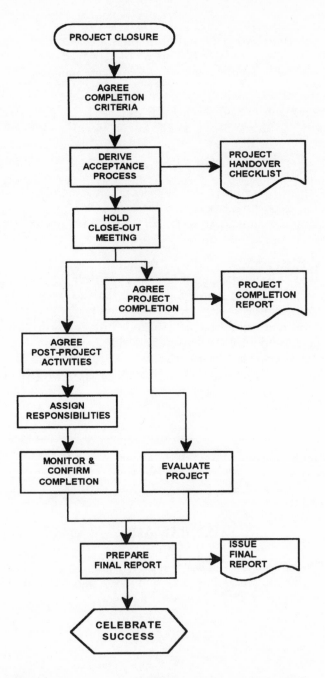

Figure 9.2 *Process flow diagram — Project closure.*

CHECKLIST 27: KEY LEADERSHIP ACTIONS DURING PROJECT CLOSURE

■ *The stakeholders:*
- Maintain regular reporting.
- Agree acceptance criteria.
- Involve end users in handover checklist design.
- Agree follow-on activities.
- Evaluate performance.
- Sign-off all reports and completion documentation.

■ *Project tasks:*
- Seek sign-off of work breakdown structure.
- Review outstanding issues.
- Agree action plans for issues.
- Confirm all action plans implemented and complete.
- Update the project records and file.

■ *Project team:*
- Maintain regular team meetings.
- Maintain participation and consult regularly.
- Anticipate risks and issues that hinder closure.
- Review team performance.
- Identify valuable learning points.
- Reward team performance.

■ *Team members:*
- Confirm all responsibilities fulfilled satisfactorily.
- Appraise performance.
- Advise additional training needs.
- Recognise and reward performance.
- Seek opportunities for further development.

Celebrate your success!

10

Using a Computer

In common with many business processes today, the management of projects can benefit from using computer technology. A project is controlled and managed through the collection and use of information to take decisions and software exists to help the project manager in this process. A wide range of project management software is available ranging from a modest investment to very expensive. The explosion in graphic interface programs has made the use of computers more accessible to everyone, making the software easier to use and understand.

It is important to remember that computer software is a tool to help you manage the project from start to finish. It is not just a planning tool, although this is a popular misunderstanding. The critical path techniques today are developed to enable you to plan, schedule and control your project and computer software is based on these fundamental processes. The modern computer gives you access to some sophisticated techniques as a serious or casual user in programs that until recently were the domain of information systems gurus. However, there is one thing the computer cannot do for you. It cannot review your wealth of experience, select appropriate information, make a judgement and take the decision. The computer can only take decisions based on the information you input to the program; if this data is wrong then the resulting output is also at fault. Yet because it comes from the computer people fall into the trap of believing the output – because the computer must be right! The critical problem is to make sure the correct data is given to the computer initially which is easy to say, not so easy always to enact.

One of the most valuable features of all project management software is the speed and ease of reporting a large amount of data in excellent formats. This makes a significant contribution to reducing the time to take decisions in support of the control process. Most software allows you to select the data you want to report and design the formats to suit your particular needs.

WHAT CAN SOFTWARE DO?

Much of the processing of information in the derivation of a plan and schedule can be effectively carried out with the advantage of rapid output of the results. It is quite common to find this software just being used to produce a Gantt chart at the start of a project. A presentable chart, that looks good and is easy to understand helps to explain to management and others what is intended to happen in a project. This is only the beginning but to go any further requires an understanding of the more complex features of the software.

These programs are really a combination of a graphics, spreadsheet and database program to make a complex operating system for managing all aspects of the project. The graphics part produces the Gantt chart, the logic diagram or PERT chart and the graphs used for reporting. The spreadsheet part is used for the forms, tables and reports produced using the available data. The database part stores and manipulates the data provided for calculation, using the spreadsheet section to insert results into the tables, charts and diagrams viewed on screen. This combination gives the software a huge range of features to assist the project process. The difficulty is the learning curve to understand such complex software and remember how to use the many features without having to resort to the reference manual every time!

During the early part of the project it is relatively easy to input the essential planning data to generate a Gantt chart and insert the resources. You spend much of your time becoming familiar with the software. Then you move into the execution phase and have less time to use the program. You are probably only going to update the schedule once a week or even less frequently and then the reference manual starts to become well thumbed! It is easy to forget how to use the many features provided for control unless you use them on a very regular basis. Time to update is often a major aspect of using software that is ignored in the plan. You need more time than you expect to input the reported progress and update the information stored in the program. This is even more of a problem if the team members are not involved or do not have familiarity with the software. If the updating is completely your responsibility it is quite possible you will rapidly fall behind with the inputting of information. The program is then so out of date that it has no added value for you and then acquires an unwarranted reputation. People start to complain that it is too complex, time-consuming and difficult to use.

So treat the software as a tool in your toolkit. If the tool fits the job in hand, make good use of it but make sure everyone in the team is given adequate training. Not everyone is comfortable with using computers or complex software. If you believe there is a value for your project encourage and facilitate the learning process. Most software programs are designed around some fundamental features that include:

- tabulating a list of tasks at different levels of the WBS;
- inputting duration data;
- inputting the dependency information;
- calculating the critical path and float data;
- deriving the Gantt chart;
- deriving the logic diagram or PERT chart;
- inputting a list of resources;
- assignment of resources by responsibility or capacity;
- inputting of cost data as resource cost rates and materials costs;
- deriving budget and cost curves, calculating earned value;
- scheduling the project based on the input data;
- 'what-if' analysis of issues using the Gantt chart;
- reassignment of resources;
- identifying and correcting resource overloads;
- outputting a wide range of reports.

All programs handle the data in a slightly different way and include many other features to allow the optimisation of the schedule in detail.

Throughout this book you are encouraged to record essential data about the project at each step of the project process. Most of the templates suggested for this purpose normally appear in all software as default tables although the layout and data formats may vary slightly. Some programs give the user considerable freedom to design these tables to present the data in a format you desire, an important element when selecting software.

Using a software program

Most programs give you a number of different ways to input information and build the project plan. Each program gives you a recommended approach to use but this is not restricted. Flexibility is important and you are certain to be more comfortable with a program that works the way you think. The steps involved follow a sequence:

- Open a new project file.
- Insert project title, start date and project manager's name.
- Set up the master calendar giving public and organisational holidays.
- If possible, design the specific formats for the tables you require.
- Input the project organisation – the core team on a resource listing.
- Set up resource calendars – one for yourself and each team member to show their available capacity for the project, including holidays.
- Input the list of key stages to a blank Gantt chart.
- Assign responsibilities for the key stages – select by responsibility; if capacity is used the schedule is automatically adjusted when durations are added unless more than one person is assigned. Beware shared responsibility!
- Input the durations for each key stage.
- Input the dependencies between the key stages.
- Program calculates the critical path, the key stage start and finish times and floats.
- Gantt chart produced, highlighting critical key stages.
- PERT diagram produced.
- Table generated showing early and late start and finish times with total float.
- Total project time is now available.
- Input cost data as resource cost rates and materials costs for key stages.
- Operating budget cumulative curve calculated.

You do not have to input cost data if cost control features are not used. This process gives you the base plan ready for optimisation using the approach discussed earlier. Most programs use a default condition of 'finish' to 'start' for all dependencies. You have the option to:

- use an alternative condition – 'start' to 'start' or 'finish' to 'finish';
- 'fix' a start or finish date – it cannot move under any circumstances and is sometimes known as a 'must date';
- introduce 'lags' and 'leads' – with caution.

When you have optimised the schedule to arrive at an acceptable completion date you can explore the detailed work inside each key stage. Use the template suggested in Chapter 7 to derive the data and responsibilities, then update the program as the work plan becomes a commitment by everyone concerned. To input this information you need to:

- add extended team members to a resource list;
- ideally create resource calendars for each – otherwise the program assumes each is 100 per cent available;
- add the task list at the lower levels in the relevant key stage on the Gantt chart;
- input the duration data;
- insert dependencies between the tasks;
- assign each task – by responsibility or capacity;
- update cost rate data for new resources assigned.

The program alerts you to any resource overloads created in assignment by capacity. If a person is assigned to work when they are listed on their calendar as not being available, or they are committed to an earlier assignment, two options are available:

- assign another;
- extend the task duration on the schedule to a listed availability.

The consequence may be an extension of the project completion date and further optimisation is necessary by reiteration at key stage or lower levels of the plan. This is where the computer is powerful because of its speed at looking at the options available to take a decision. 'What-if' analysis allow you to quickly review the impact of moving or extending tasks, moving or adjusting resource assignments and changing the plan. Always check the consequences of these reiterations – the critical path may change.

When you have an acceptable schedule freeze this as the baseline for control. Make sure everyone is issued with copies of the detail and keep copies of everything in the project file. Once you have frozen the baseline it is prudent to keep a copy of the project file under a separate name as a back-up in case someone resets the baseline without your knowledge!

The next phase of the project, doing the work, provides you with feedback of what is happening. This data is inputted to the program using the 'update mode' where percentage completion is given to each active task up to the current date. Remember that the task is regarded as linear and it is better to calculate the percentage. Obtain the forecast of time required to complete and decide if the task duration is extended into the float zone or further. The task bar can then show a true position, the percentage complete and the time to complete with a realistic completion date.

Updating the schedule task by task takes time to accomplish and programs do vary in the features they offer and restrictions built in to make this process easy to complete. Any conflicts concerning resource assignments that arise from updating the progress are alerted, so you can take corrective action. Then you can explore the options available to view the impact on the rest of the outstanding work and take informed decisions.

WHAT SOFTWARE DOES NOT DO

The computer software works entirely on data you supply. Intuitive decision processing is beyond its capability so there are some aspects of the work of a project that are entirely dependent on people:

- deciding the deliverables and benefits;
- identifying tasks and key stages;
- deciding the dependencies between key stages and the tasks inside,
- deciding the resources available to work on the project;
- doing the project work;
- identifying risks to the project;
- ranking of risks and allocating responsibilities for managing risks;
- reviewing the project risk log;
- deriving a milestone schedule;
- identifying issues – process and technical;
- problem-solving;
- action planning to solve problems;
- resolving conflicts;
- monitoring and tracking the project activities;
- measuring project progress;
- reporting project progress.

These activities represent the major part of the project activity so keep the project driving the software and do not allow the software to drive the project. The document templates suggested for status reports, risk and issue management are not included in most project software packages. You can easily construct these using existing word processors or spreadsheet programs. Experience with cost control suggests that setting up cost data and records using a spreadsheet is easy to accomplish, accurate and quickly updated.

Software cannot ever replace the essential human inputs to project activity or the building and motivation of an effective team. The combined brain power and experience of an effective team is far greater than the sum of the individual parts and surpasses the power of any computer software for project management.

SELECTING PROJECT SOFTWARE

Selecting software for project management is emotive in most organisations. Unless your organisation is very focused on project activity with a defined software policy the selection process causes untold controversy and conflict. Everyone has their own favourite package for the work they do and even the same software is configured to operate differently according to individual needs. Perhaps the information systems department will review available programs and make a selection that becomes policy. Experienced people with a record of success managing projects are the best to review software and decide if it is a valuable tool to make the job easier for the type of projects undertaken. Some packages are particularly suited to certain types of projects so selection should not be based on price alone but include a review of:

- past track record of performance;
- ease of use;
- compatibility with other software in use;
- stand-alone or networked and availability;
- platforms available;
- features for planning and scheduling;
- features for control and updating;
- quality and ease of reporting;
- networking features – passwords, access restrictions, etc;
- training available;
- help line and back-up available.

Project software is complex so it is often the product of specialist suppliers, rather than just the major software suppliers who are household names in the industry. There is little evidence to show there are compatibility problems with such specialist packages and many are available on demonstration disks.

If you are selecting a software package then seek expert help and review what is available. Compile a list of things you want from the program then review the feature lists to decide which program to put on test. Do not restrict this list too much. As you gain in experience and confidence you expect more from your software and a change later is expensive.

POSTSCRIPT

So you have come to the end of this project – has it been a success? You will only really know when you apply the techniques and processes suggested here. All are tried and proven and there is nothing astoundingly new or reactionary in these techniques. This project has been focused on deriving a step by step process to help you achieve success with your projects in future, giving you tips to improve based on personal experience. If you do achieve success and feel more in control of your working life as a project manager, then the work of this project has been a success. If you have any interesting experiences to relate using the approaches given here, the author will be pleased to hear from you via the publisher.

APPENDIX 1
GLOSSARY OF TERMS

There is a considerable amount of jargon used by project managers today, enhanced by the rapid growth in the use of personal computers for planning and control of projects. The list gives some of the more common terms and their usual meaning.

Activity. A clearly defined task or tasks with known duration: usually a group of tasks which together complete a particular step or part of the work.

Activity on node diagram. A network diagram where all activities are represented by the node or event, usually as a box, and the arrows are used merely to show the logical flow of the project.

ACWP. The actual recorded cost, including costs committed, of the work actually performed up to a particular point in the project schedule.

Backward pass. The procedure by which the latest event times or the finish and start times for the activities of a network are determined.

Bar chart. A graphical presentation of the activities of a project derived from the project logic diagram shown as a timed schedule.

Baseline plan. The final 'frozen' plan as signed off by the sponsor before implementation. This is also the recorded plan, against which all progress is measured and variances analysed and reported.

BCWP. The budgeted cost, based on the operating budget, of the work that is actually completed up to a particular point in the project schedule.

BCWS. The budgeted cost, based on the operating budget, of the work that is planned to be completed up to a particular point in the project schedule.

Benefit. A measurable gain from the project that is a primary underlying reason for the project being initiated.

Change request. A standard format form to record and request approval from the key stakeholders for a significant change to the baseline plan.

Control system. The procedures established at the start of the project that provide the leader with the necessary data to compare planned status with the actual status at any instant in time, to identify variances and to take corrective action.

Cost control diagram. A graphical representation of the actual and budgeted costs of the work actually performed against the scheduled and budgeted costs of the work planned.

Cost variance. The difference between the value of the work actually performed (BCWP) and the actual costs incurred and committed (ACWP).

Critical activity. Any activity in the project that has been analysed to show it has zero float and must therefore be completed on time if the project is not to slip.

Critical path. The sequence of activities which determines the total time for the project. All activities on the critical path are known as citical ativities.

Deliverable. A specific, defined, measurable and tangible output from the project. Most projects have several deliverables.

Dependency. The basic rule of logic governing logic diagram and network drawing – any activity which is dependent on another is normally shown to emerge from the head event of the activity on which it depends.

Duration. The estimated or actual time to complete an activity.

EET. The earliest event time – the earliest completion time for an event which does not effect the total project time.

EFT. The earliest finish time of an activity without changing total time or the spare or float time.

Elapsed time. The duration of a piece of the work expressed in real, calendar working days – taking into account holidays, weekends, etc not worked.

EST. The earliest start time of an activity.

Event. A point in the progress of the project after total completion of all preceding activities.

Float. Difference between the time necessary and the time available for an activity.

Forward pass. The procedure for determining the earliest event times of a network.

Gantt chart. A graphical method of showing a project schedule which shows project time, dates, all activities, resources and their relationships. It is derived from the logic diagram when it has been analysed for float.

Issue. A risk to the project, or an unforeseen event that has become a reality and needs to be resolved if the project integrity is not to be threatened.

Issue log. A sequential listing of all issues raised during the life of a project with essential information about their handling.

Key stage. A group of closely related activities that can be isolated together as a clear stage of the project which must be complete before passing to the next stage.

Lag. An intentional delay period of time introduced between two activities in a logic diagram.

Layering the plan. See multi-level planning.

Lead. A specific amount of time a successor activity should start after the start of its predecessor even though the predecessor is not complete.

LET. The latest time by which an event can be achieved without affecting the total project time from start to finish.

LFT. The latest possible finish time without changing the total task or float times.

Logic diagram. A graphic representation of the activities in a project with clearly identified logical dependencies established.

LRC. The linear responsibility chart that displays a complete listing of key stages and/or activities with the names of the resource(s) who have been allocated responsibility for each as part of the plan.

LST. The latest possible time an activity can start without affecting the total project time.

Milestone. Another name for an event, but usually reserved for a significant or major event in the project. Often used for identifying key progress reporting points.

Monitoring. The process of checking what is happening and collecting data on project progress.

Multi-level planning. Planning the project at several levels of detail, starting with the key stages and then exploding each key stage to show all the associated activities. Where necessary any activity is further exploded to show further detail of associated tasks at the next level down and so on.

Must date. A planned date when an activity or group of activities must be complete under all circumstances.

PERT diagram. The logic diagram in the PERT (Programme Evaluation Review Technique) project control system.

Predecessor. The activity immediately prior to an event.

Project approved budget. The budget approved at the conception of the project, based on outline plans only with contingency included.

Project file. A central file that must contain copies of all documentation, letters, faxes, etc relating to the project. It is the project archive and the basis for subsequent evaluation and continuous improvement activities.

Project lifecycle. A systems approach to a project where the project is described as passing through four phases from conception to termination.

Project log book. A bound A4 book with numbered pages where the project leader records all events, action plans and project activities. It comprises a complete event record cross-referenced to the project file. On larger projects each team member should also maintain a project log book.

Project operating budget. The budget derived at operating level after detailed planning to first or preferably the second level is completed.

Project steering team. A senior management committee often made up of project sponsors who have the power to prioritise and steer projects in the direction necessary to meet corporate objectives.

Resource. Anything other than time which is needed for carrying out an activity but most commonly restricted to people involved in the project.

Resource levelling. Utilisation of available float within a network to ensure that resources required are appreciably constant.

Resource smoothing. The scheduling of activities within the limits of their total floats to minimise fluctuations in resource requirements.

Risk. An event that has been identified as potentially threatening the project integrity if it actually happens.

Risk log. A sequential listing of all risks identified throughout the project life and information about their ranking, probability and management.

Schedule. The project plan converted to 'real time' against a calendar by inserting realistic agreed time estimates and resource capacity factors into all the project activities.

Schedule variance. The difference between the value of the work completed (BCWP) and the budgeted cost, from the operating budget, of the work planned to be completed at a particular point in the schedule.

Single person day. A method of estimating activity durations using 100 per cent capacity for an individual to carry out the work. It represents a full working day but in estimating ignores holidays etc.

Soft project. A project where the objectives are only broadly stated and the resources needed are unknown and flexible, the scope left open intentionally and deadlines not defined clearly.

Sponsor. The senior manager who takes ownership of the project on behalf of the organisation.

Stakeholder. Any individual who has an interest or stake in the project at any time during the project lifecycle.

Successor. The activity immediately following an event.

Task. A specific defined piece of work usually carried out by one person in a finite measurable time. A sub-unit of a project activity.

Time limited scheduling. The scheduling of activities such that the specified project time is not exceeded using resources to a predetermined pattern.

Total float. The total spare time possessed by an activity beyond the estimated duration.

Tracking. The process of taking progress information gathered in a control system and inserting this into the original plan to show the actual status, ie the compliance or deviation from the planned status of the project at that point in time.

Work breakdown structure. The diagrammatic presentation of all the key stages and their associated activities arranged in a hierarchical format, showing each level of planning.

Work plan. A standard format form or chart for recording an agreed listing of the tasks to be carried out by an individual or department, complete with agreed start and finish times for each within the overall project schedule.

APPENDIX 2
FURTHER READING

Barker, Alan (1993) *Making Meetings Work*, The Industrial Society, London.

Cleland, David I and King, William R (1988) *Project Management Handbook*, Van Nostrand Reinhold, New York.

Crawley, John (1992) *Constructive Conflict Management*, Nicholas Brealey, London.

Davenport, Jenny and Lipton, Gordon (1993) *Communications for Managers*, The Industrial Society, London.

Eales-White, Rupert (1992) *The Power of Persuasion*, Kogan Page, London.

Frame, Davidson J (1994) *The New Project Management*, Jossey-Bass Inc, San Francisco.

Hardingham, Alison and Royal, Jenny (1994) *Pulling Together: Teamwork in Practice*, Institute of Personnel and Development, London.

Hurst, Bernice (1996) *The Handbook of Communication Skills*, 2nd edition, Kogan Page, London.

Kindler, Herbert S (1990) *Risk Taking*, Kogan Page, London (out of print).

Lockyear, Keith (1984) *Critical Path Analysis and Other Project Network Techniques*, Pitman Publishing, London.

Pokras, S (1989) *Successful Problem Solving and Decision Making*, Kogan Page, London.

Rosenau, M D (1991) *Successful Project Management*, Van Nostrand Reinhold, New York.

Senge, P (1990) *The Fifth Discipline*, Doubleday, New York.

Stewart, Dorothy M (ed) (1990) *Handbook of Management Skills*, Gower Publishing Co, London.

Vincent, Geoff (1988) *Taming Technology: How to Manage a Development Project*, British Institute of Management, London.

Young, Trevor L (1993) *Leading Projects*, The Industrial Society, London.

INDEX

acceptance process 186
accountability 31
action cycle 20, 21
action plan 156, 161
active evaluation 190
activity 88, 211
ACWP 180, 211
administration 143
agenda for kick-off meeting 52
allocating responsibility 95, 96
analysing, resource requirements 113
analysing the critical path 104
analysis
  logic diagram 107
  what-if 205
approval, launch 117
authority 30

BAC 180
back-tracking 174
baseline plan 118, 152, 205
BCWP 180, 211
BCWS 180, 211
budget 117

cause and effect analysis 159
change 13,14
change request 135
changes to plan 128, 133
close-out meeting 187
closing 185
communication 128
completion 153
  criteria for 186

handover checklist 187
completion report 188,189
computer, using 201
concurrent activities 88
conflict 165
  managing 168
  resolving 168
  and risks 167
  types 167
constraints 50
contingencies 101
control system 141, 212
  checklist 144
  design 141
control, costs 179
controlling costs 178
core team 46
corrective action, checklist for 157
  taking 156
cost control diagram 181, 212
cost measures 180
costs 204
  controlling 178
criteria for completion 186
critical path 103, 212
  analysing 104
  identifying 103, 114
critical success factors 127
CSF 127
  process 127
  project 127
customer 46, 134
  contract 50
  needs and expectations 48

customer *contd.*
  satisfaction 47
CV 181

data gathering 158
defining the project 63
deliverable 212
dependency 90, 112, 212
documentation 55, 64
duration 98, 99, 103, 212
durations, estimating 99
dynamic life-cycle 19, 20

effort 98
escalation of issues 149
estimate, definition 98
estimating, contingencies 101
  durations 99
  people problems 100
evaluating your project 190
evaluation, active 190
  asking questions 190, 191, 192
  post project 190, 191, 193
  technical 194, 195
execution, process flow diagram
  183

feudal kingdoms 175
fishbone diagram 159
float 106, 110, 114, 213
forecasting, completion 154, 155
forgotten tasks 154
FTC 180

Gantt chart 107, 111, 115, 121, 124,
  125, 152, 202, 204, 213
glossary of terms 211

handover, checklist 187

identifying needs and expectations
  49
issue management form 150, 151
issue status log 148, 213
issues 77, 124, 127, 130, 213
  escalation 149
  managing 148

ranking 148
responsibility for escalated 150

key stages 88, 93, 94, 106, 114, 117,
  121, 122, 213
  costs 117
key stage owner 95, 114, 121, 125
key stage responsibility Chart 97
key stage work plans 121, 122
key stakeholders 34, 127, 134
kick-off meeting 51
KSO 95, 114

lag 107, 213
launch
  approval to 117
  meeting 134, 136
launching the project 121
lead 107, 213
life-cycle 19, 20
log book 58, 165
logic diagram 90, 93, 104, 107,
  213
  analysis 107

managing conflict 168
  the dynamic life-cycle 38
  issues 148
  performance 38
  stakeholders 36, 37
  time 169
matrix, working 173
measures, cost control 180
meeting, launch 134, 136
  close-out 187
meetings 132
  1:1 177
  frequency 145
milestones 112, 130, 214
  schedule 124, 126
monitoring and tracking, checklist
  155
monitoring process 146
  progress 143

needs and expectations 48
node 105

optimising, schedule 114
organisation chart 56

people problems (estimating) 100
PERT 104, 105, 107, 202, 204, 214
plan 118
post project
    appraisal 196
    evaluation 190, 191, 193
problem solving 157
problem statement 161
progress meetings 161
    checklist for 163
    monitoring 143
    reporting 164
project
    baseline plan 152
    benefits 127, 196
    brief 59, 67, 68
    budget, review 117
    changes, handling 133
    characteristics 17
    closing 185
    closure, flow diagram 198
    completion 153
    constraints 50
    control system 140
    core team 46
    costs 204
    costs, controlling 178
    customer 46
    definition, checklist for approval
        81
    definition 16, 80
    definition approval 80
    deliverables 127
    documentation 55, 64
    drift 185
    end users 46
    evaluation 190
    execution, flow diagram 183
    extended team 47
    file 55, 164, 214
    file contents 165
    issue management form 150,
        151
    Issue status log 148

key stages 88, 93, 94, 106, 114
key stages, identifying 89
key stages, using 89
key stakeholders 34
launching 121
leader 31
    qualities of 32
leadership 35
    three dimensions 36
life-cycle 19, 20
log book 58, 165, 214
logic diagram 90, 107
    rules for deriving 93
management 21
manager role 25, 29
newsletter 191
objectives 127
operating budget 117, 214
organisation chart 56
planning 85, 87
progress meetings 161
records 164
risk log 73, 74, 115
    review 116
risks, review of 147
sources 18
specification 59, 69
sponsor 28, 29, 45, 116, 117, 134
stakeholder list 174
stakeholders 30, 34, 35
starting up 45
status reports 129, 130, 131
steering team 28, 29, 214
structure 27
team 134
tracking 150
work breakdown structure 93

ranking issues 149
records 154
report, completion 188, 189
reporting 128
    progress 164
reports, frequency 145
resolving conflict 168
resource requirements 113

responsibilities
  project manager 29
  project sponsor 29
  project steering team 29
responsibility 30
  allocating 95, 96
  escalated issues 150
  recording 95, 97
risk, actions 76
risk assessment 73
  checklist for 79
risk log, review 73, 74, 115, 116, 215
risk management 69, 71
  form 78, 116
  why? 71
risks, ranking 75, 76
risks, ranking definitions 76
risks 124, 127, 215
  checklist for review 147
  impact 75
  matrix 75
  probability 75
  review of 147

schedule 98, 215
  optimising 114
scope of work 60, 70
selecting team members 40
series activities 88
SMART test 68, 69, 125
software, features 203
software, project management 201
  selecting 207
  using 203
SOW 70

specification 59, 69
sponsor 116, 117, 215
stakeholder list 64, 66, 174
stakeholders 30, 34, 35, 36, 37, 127, 215
  managing 36
status report form 131
status reports 129, 130, 131
steps, problem solving 159
SV 181

taking corrective action 156
task 88, 215
  forgotten 154
taskboarding 90
team 46, 47, 134
team building 41
teamwork 39
technical evaluation 194, 195
time limited scheduling 102, 215
time management, actions to improve 170
  barriers to 171
  checklist for 178
time, managing 169
total float 106, 110, 114, 215
tracking 150, 216

using PERT data 107

what-if analysis 205
work breakdown structure 93, 114, 117, 127, 216
work plans 121, 122, 216
working in a matrix 173

INDEX OF CHECKLISTS

1. Identifying and managing stakeholders 37
2. Managing performance 38
3. Selecting team members 40
4. Actions for effective leadership 44
5. Identifying customer needs 49
6. Project kick-off meeting 53
7. Leadership actions during project start-up 62
8. Questions for risk assessment 79
9. Developing the definition 81
10. Key leadership actions during project definition 83
11. Deriving the project logic diagram 93
12. Some guidelines for allocating ownership 96
13. A baseline plan checklist 118
14. Key leadership actions during project planning 120
15. The project launch meeting 136
16. Key leadership actions during project launch 138
17. Designing the control system 144
18. Reviewing project risks 147
19. Monitoring and tracking 155
20. Taking corrective action 157
21. Project progress meetings 163
22. Encouraging good time management 178
23. Key leadership actions during project execution 184
24. Active evaluation 191
25. Post-project evaluation 193
26. Technical evaluation 195
27. Key leadership actions during project closure 199

INDEX OF PROCESS FLOW DIAGRAMS

Figure 4.3   Process flow diagram – project start-up   61
Figure 5.7   Process flow diagram – project definition   82
Figure 6.11   Process flow diagram – project planning   119
Figure 7.6   Process flow diagram – project launch   137
Figure 8.9   Process flow diagram – project execution   183
Figure 9.2   Process flow diagram – project closure   198